Yotti Yotta Memories

Yotti Yotta Memories

Tess De Araugo

ARCADIA

First published 2016 by Arcadia, the general books' imprint of
Australian Scholarly Publishing Pty Ltd
7 Lt Lothian St North, North Melbourne, Victoria 3051
www.scholarly.info / enquiries@scholarly.info / (61) (3) 93296963

ISBN 978-1-925333-44-2

Contents

Preface

Who knows exactly how many thousands of years the Murray River has meandered and churned its way across southern Australia? It is the second largest river in Australia, and runs for 2575 kilometers (1600 miles) from its rising in the New South Wales Snowy Mountains to the seas in South Australia. The tribal people of different groups knew the Murray at various points along its winding course as Milliwa, Mille, Fingola, Tangula, Tongala.

Groups of Aborigines belonging to the Yotti Yotta tribe lived along the river in the Barmah, Echuca, Gunbower areas, with their country running west to approximately Cohuna, which was the tribal boundary of the Barapaapa. The Yotti Yotta line of ownership continued to Deniliquin where it was met by Jeithi country. The Kwat Kwat tribes people held the land to the east of the Yotti Yotta, with the Bangerang also on the eastern boundary. Their land stretched to the south of the Yotti Yotta territory. North of the Murray, the Pikkolatpan tribe spoke of the Bangerang as the Yoorta (variously spelt Yotti Yotta, Yorti Yorta, Jotti Jotta), and approximately ten groups spoke or understood the Yotti Yotta language.

In 1824, Hamilton Hume (Australian born son of a superintendent of convicts) and William Hovell (English born) led the first exploring party to reach the Murray River and named it the Hume. The tall, well-built tribesmen they met wore possum skin cloaks; the women too were dressed in possum skins. Six years later, Captain Charles Sturt reached the river, and not knowing it was the Hume (now known as the upper Murray), called it the Murray after the Colonial Secretary. Squatters followed explorers to claim the land and it was at Towong, north-east of Corryong, that a tribal woman was presented with a breast-plate by settlers, inscribed 'Kitty Howcarley, Queen of Towwong, Hume River.'

By 1834, the Aborigines in the Port Phillip District of New South Wales, later known as Victoria, were losing their land to white men. As the years progressed, hundreds of tribal people lost their lives in battles of defence; they were murdered; they died in prisons; diseases contracted from the white population sent thousands of tribal people to their graves. The estimated 17,000 Aborigines all lost their own territories to the white race and the introduced stock.

During the years of the take-over, the tribes people lived where they hoped to find safety and food. Fortunate were the groups – permitted by the squatter or settler – to camp on their own previously owned land. Revelations concerning the lives of the Aborigines before white settlement, and during the early stages, have been, in many instances, handed down orally through the generations, from tribal forebears to thousands of people of Aboriginal descent in Victoria. This information is being recorded.

Tess De Araugo

Part One

Some Aborigines of the Murray Valley

Chapter One

Nimble Dick and Lananglie

In 1864 the *Riverine Herald* published a series of accounts of tribal life told to an unnamed English settler by a tribesman of the Murray River. White men called him Nimble Dick. The Englishman wrote of:

'An old fellow who changed a fearfully long and unpronounceable Aboriginal name for that of Nimble Dick; and though his hair had been for some time white, and his cheeks sunk, he well deserved the name. His eye was bright, his limbs still strong and supple, and altogether he was more hale and active than many a much younger man of his tribe. He was very voluble in his speech, but fortunately understood English well though he spoke it in a manner with which we shall not trouble the readers.

'Lananglie was Nimble Dick's wife. She hobbled about the camp leaning heavily for support on her yarn stick, which she held with both hands, her body almost bent double. She was so thin, 'you could count every bone.' Her hair was white and her face and forehead very wrinkled. She appeared to the settler to be about sixty years old. Nimble Dick spoke of her:

'My old wife has got a bullet in her leg now; she was shot many years ago. She was a fine girl once, and she's not as old as she looks. She is many summers younger than me but she has suffered terribly. She has been waddied and speared I don't know how many times by Blacks, and shot twice by Whites. It was a pity, for when she was young she was quick like a wallaby and never quiet – always laughing. Everyone said then, "That is the best lubra in a good many tribes".

'Lananglie's brother gave her away to the chief of another tribe when she was quite a piccaninny, in exchange for this elder's grown-up daughter. Lananglie lived with her father and mother until she was old enough to be married to the chief. When this man wanted her she was still very young. Lananglie's brother would not let him have her unless he gave him another lubra. The one he had been given before had grown old and ugly.

'The two tribes had a fight about it but our tribe beat the other and kept Lananglie a good while longer. The other tribe sent men to watch for her, and they caught her when she was out from the camp a good way, digging yams with some other lubras. The other women ran home and told of it and her brother and four or five of us went after her. We overtook the men and were taking her away from them before they could get into their own country. We had a fight and when they saw we were beating them, they speared Lananglie in her side.

'After that fight, Lananglie always liked me and after a while I liked her and we said we would be married but she was my cousin and a Blackfellow must not marry his relation of any woman of his own tribe. He must steal or buy one, or get one given to him out of another tribe.

'The chief that wanted Lananglie sent word to her brother that he would give him another young lubra for her. Her brother told her she must go but she only laughed at him and said she would not and for a long time he tried to persuade her. She always shook her head and laughed and he got angry. One day in a great rage he hit her on the head with a stone tomahawk and cut the bone open to the brain. When she fell down, he beat her with a heavy waddy and I believe some of her ribs were broken.

'A long time she was sick and when she was getting well he told her once more she must go to the other tribe but she said 'no' and her brother threw her on the fire and she nearly burned to death. The old men of our tribe then said Lananglie must go.

'I spoke to her about it and said, "Lananglie, when you are strong and able to walk a good way we will run away from the tribe and live a good way off in the ranges by ourselves." She was glad to hear me speak like that and said what I was thinking of was all right. I told her to keep on talking about the other tribe and how much she wanted to go away because she was afraid her brother would kill her. She did that and the old men and her brother all thought she wanted to do as she asked. They sent messengers to the chief and told him his wife would go to him as soon as she was well. He believed them and sent the lubra he had promised to Lananglie's brother.

'When three moons were gone, Lananglie could walk but was still weak. There was a great corroboree a good way off and almost all of the tribes were to go. They left a sick camp – some old men that could not walk so far and women that were not well. Two fighting men stopped at this camp because of their lubras and picanninies so that they could take care of them. Lananglie and I said, 'This is the time that we will get away and not come back to the tribe anymore.'

'I told my cousin, Toolambel, what we would do and he said he would help me but when the time came, the elders made him go to the corroboree because he was a good singer and knew a good deal about the dances. I went with the men half-way, then turned back. In the night I returned to the camp where Lananglie was and, as we had arranged, I cried out like a mopoke and she came out when she heard me. The people were all asleep. We walked away towards the steep ranges.

'Lananglie was very glad but still very weak and she could not walk far at a time. She sat down often and cried, and by morning we had not gone far away from the camp. I carried her into a scrubby place and we hid there all day. When it was nearly dark we went on a little and then Lananglie cried and said she was thirsty. We had no water with us so I went on to get some in a wallaby skin that I had at a creek some way off. When I came back I could not find Lananglie. It was dark so I could not see any tracks. I coo-eed, soft at first and then as loud as I could but no answer came. I hunted about the forest but I could not make out what had become of her.

'Just before daylight I fell asleep. I woke to feel something tight around my throat and I thought it must be a snake it felt so cold. I was afraid to move and lay there a long time half stupid. I could feel the breath of something on my face and the thing moved and I knew it was alive. I could not stand it any longer. The sweat was pouring down from my head and blinding me so that when I tried to look I could not see. I made up my mind and all of a sudden I gave a great spring and leaped to my feet, wiped the sweat from my eyes and looked about. I said, 'I have had a great dream,' and I looked round and I saw the fires I had made in the night. Then I saw Lananglie lying on the ground and it was her arm that had been round my neck. Although I had jumped up in that way, I had not waked her.

'She was very fast asleep but shivering with cold. I brought fire and warmed her and after a while she woke and told me she thought I was a good while getting the water so she tried to follow me. She was afraid to be alone. She went on a little way and her head got giddy and she fell down, and fainted I suppose. In a good while she came to her senses and saw the fires I had made and she crawled towards them, looking everywhere for me, and when she saw me asleep on the ground, she fell down by me.

'You may think this is not worth listening to but if a white man lost his young wife all night and thought he had a snaked round his neck in the morning, then found it was his wife's arm, he'd think it was worth telling, my word. I often think about it and how glad we were that morning – until we began to think the smoke from my big fires would be seen a long way.

'"We must go on," Lananglie said, and I said so too, but she was weak and I was tired. We started out though because it was very dangerous to stay where we were. There was a glen in the mountains where there was a spring. The tribe did not often go there and I had only been once when I was a little boy, so that was where we wanted to hide. We walked on and on very slowly and sometimes I carried Lananglie a little way. About dinner time she said she must sleep, so we both lay down in a thick brushy and grassy place and slept for I don't know how long.

'Lananglie woke me, pulling at me and shaking me, saying there were Blacks on our tracks. She had just seen a dog and said it was a Black's dog. I told her it must have been a wild dog but she insisted it was not a warragul but a tribesman's own dog. Soon she saw him again and pointed to it. The dog was some distance away and running a scent. I could see it was not a wild dog and was sure some Blacks must be near. We looked around very carefully and could see nothing but the dog still hunting about, but in a short time we heard a low coo-ee. There was no mistake about that and it was not far off. I thought the men from the sick camp must be following us at first but the dog was a strange one that I had never seen before. I smothered up the little fire we had with earth and ashes. It was of no use moving. In a few steps we would be in pretty clear ground where we could be seen from a distance. We kept quite still but I could hear Lananglie's heart beating. It can't make that noise now, poor thing.

'Well I got up in a tree to have a look and a short distance off I saw a heavy smoke signal rising about the trees. Soon it was answered by another one a long way off. I knew then that those nearest us were calling up other tribesmen behind them. I could tell by the distance between the smokes that they could not get up to the others before dark and I reckoned the first ones would camp where they were for the night and wait for them next morning. I was sure they were following our tracks as they must have seen my fires of the night before. It was a strange dog we had seen. I knew the tribesmen must be from some other country. Whoever they were, I felt certain I should be killed, and Lananglie taken away.

'Nimble Dick spoke a few words to the old woman, Lananglie, who was nodding off to sleep. She sprang up with an agility that was surprising in one of her appearance, yabbered vehemently, and stood almost erect for a moment. Sinking down again as if half-exhausted by the effort, she patted Dick's cheek and muttered something in a sort of playful tone and the story-telling came to an end.

'"Don't tell any more this time,"Lananglie said to her husband.'

Chapter Two

Emu and Pelican Totems

Peter Beveridge held thousands of acres of land in the Murray district in 1861 and wrote of tribal customs, languages and mythology. One story told to him by tribal people concerns the emu, the sun and creation; the Dreamtime. This story was told by tribes along the Murray with slightly differing versions. As Nimble Dick spoke of himself as an Emu man, the legend needs to be told here.

'The Tati Tati tribe occupied the country opposite Euston, on the Victorian side of the Murray. At first they were all birds and beasts and there was no sun to light up their land but they knew that a good Spirit called Gnamdenoot looked after them from above. One day two of the karwingis (emu) had a quarrel and, in great anger, one of them took the other's egg and threw it into the sky. It travelled so far it eventually reached a pile of wood which was placed there by Gnamdenoot for a special reason – to allow the karwingi egg to smash on it and break. When this happened, a large ball of fire appeared and he saw that the light coming from this was better than having darkness over the land all the time. Ever since that day, Gnamdenoot has brought light to the earth every morning.

'The Tati Tati were happy with the *nowingi* (day) now so different to *paungi* (night). They could see the holes where the *kartini* (water) was and the new *toorti* (sun) gave them both light and warmth. More changes followed. All the Tati Tati who had led good lives were rewarded. If they had collected their own food, had got on well with their neighbours and had helped their friends when they were in trouble, they were changed into Blackfellows. The *karwingi*s (emus), *purtangil*s (pelicans), *wolangi*s (possums), *goyangi*s (kangaroos) and the *gongongs* (kookaburras) all learnt to walk on the ground. The tribes people of the *karwingi* and the *purtangil* totems learnt to make and use the *patigi* (tomahawk) and the *geyami* (shield). Those who had not deserved to become human beings remained as they were forever – animals and birds.Lananglie sat on the ground beside Nimble Dick. They had returned to the settler's station to finish the story of their elopement as they had promised. After a hearty meal, Nimble Dick filled his pipe and continued.

'I stopped up in the tree watching for as long as I could see, but no one came. When I got down I began to think what was best to do. There were two lots of tribesmen as I told you, with the first lot a good way ahead of the other – and that one very close to us. I said to myself, 'Now, the first lot will wait for the second and then they will all follow on the track.' If Lananglie had been strong I would have pushed on to the mountains but it was no use to think of that. It was certain death to remain where we were. I wasn't a stupid young fellow.

'When it was dark I left Lananglie in the scrub. I was a little bit frightened about losing her again but she promised to lie still. I went out of the thick place where she was and ran about a good way, stamping my feet on the ground to make many tracks. When I was tired of that work and thought I had done enough to puzzle the trackers I went back to Lananglie and told her, 'Now we must be off.'

'Where will we go?' she asked me.

'Never mind Lananglie. I'm the fellow that won't be caught by these Pelicans.'

All the tribes have got some name. Mine is the Emu and I thought the tribesmen following us that wanted my lubra were Pelicans. I took her up in my arms and walked backwards towards where the first lot of Blacks were camped. When I was tired I put Lananglie down on a log and never let her feet touch the ground. It was hard work and very nearly I tumbled down a good many times. At last I could see their campfire through the trees but I never turned round, only looked over my shoulder. I slowed a bit to go round their camp, walking backwards, until I could see no more of the fire.

'Why did you come this way? Do you want to be killed and lose me?'

'No, my *lubra*. When they see the tracks they will say, Aha, two Blackfellows! One been hunting and one come up here to man and woman. They will see where we camped in the scrub, find the tracks I made running about, and they will be puzzled and keep looking for more tracks. Now, we must travel fast by another way to the mountains.'

'I am very weak. No use, they will find us and kill you and take me with them. Suppose many Blackfellows come, you cannot kill them all.'

'I did not know what to tell her. I made a place in the earth – a circle – and sat down in it. In a little while a thought came into my head. I went to Lananglie and asked her to stay where she was while I went away to look at the enemy camp. At first she would not let me go but I very much begged her and she said, 'Do not go too close.'

'I took my spears and *leangle* (club) and went away very softly. When I got near the tribe's fire I climbed a little way up in a tree and I saw only two Blackfellows. They were Pelicans and both young fellows. I remembered I fought one of them the time they ran away with Lananglie, and I thought if I killed the other fellow first I could beat the tribesman I knew. But how would I do that? I would wait until they were both asleep and kill them both because they would do that to me if they caught me. When the second lot of tribesmen came in the morning they would see the dead men and go back, unless there were a good many of them.

'After the tribesmen were asleep, I crawled on my hands and knees close up to their camp holding my spears, one in each hand. I crawled until I was close enough to the men to touch them, then I stood up. They were lying on their backs, close together. I lifted my arms and drove the spears into their bellies at the same time. One fellow groaned and never moved and I thought he was dead so I pulled the spear out of him to run it into the tribesman I had fought with before. But he jumped up and screamed and struggled, my first spear still hanging in his wound. He wasn't a coward and he had great strength. He caught the spear I had in my hand and I could not get it away from him. He fought like a devil. At last I tripped him up and fell on top of him and tried to strangle him.

'I did not know how near death I was then because while I was struggling with him the other fellow got up on his knees and was making a blow at my head with a stone tomahawk. It was Lananglie that saved me. When she heard the screams she ran to the camp just as the Blackfellow was going to hit me with his tomahawk. She had a fine new spear of mine in her hand and she came behind the fellow and drove it into his back. He let the tomahawk fall and dropped on his face. Lananglie sent the spear into him a good many times and he no more moved after that.

'I was so busy killing the other tribesman that I did not know about what Lananglie was doing. This Pelican bit both my arms and they bled, but I did not feel the pain for I had to kill him. Then Lananglie stooped down and took the tomahawk and beat the man with it. He soon stopped biting me. Both the Pelicans were dead and I took out their kidney fat. We burned their spears and everything else that we could not carry, and we left them there, not fit to track us anymore. We went back to our place in the scrub and when the morning came I walked about and found a big hollow tree where a person could hide. I put the *lubra* in there and covered all the tracks. It rained soon after, so no-one could see that the leaves and sticks had ever been touched. Lananglie promised to stay very quiet.

'I took my spears and climbed into a high tree a good way off from her and after a time I heard the Blacks. I knew by the noise they made they had found the dead men. Now, I thought, they will be frightened and will go. But it was not so. There were a great many tribesmen.

'I heard afterwards they were going to the mountains to knock out the front teeth of a lot of young men. There were many fighting men and young fellows amongst them. No women. They never let the *lubras* see them making the young men. The tribesmen always go a good way off in a very secret place to do it. When they have knocked out the young fellows' teeth, they are then fighting men and can eat a good many things the women and the boys must not eat. We are not allowed to tell how it is done and a Blackfellow would be killed if he spoke about the things that were done when his teeth are knocked out.

'When I heard so many voices yabbering and the noise they made, I began to be frightened. They came closer. I was very brave when I was a young fellow and not easily frightened, but I thought about the *lubra* and my heart was cold for a while. I could see them. They found our place in the scrub and scattered about looking for tracks. I didn't like the look of it.

'While I was stuck up there among the leaves of that big tree, watching the hundreds of devils that were searching for us below, I wished many things. I wished every one of them would turn into trees on a great sandy plain, without water, where no other trees could grow. I wished they would be scorched by the hot winds and covered with sand until the leaves rattled like two plates shaken together. I wished their bark would crack and their branches split for want of rain. I wished them to be always in misery by themselves, and never to die.

'I loved my *lubra*. I love her now. I hated the men that were hunting me for my life and would have taken my wife, my own young wife, and ill-used her and make her a slave. I wished I could make thunder and lightning and strike them all dead.

'Lananglie was in her early teens when she and Nimble Dick left their tribe. The settler wrote that at this stage of the story, the old tribesman stroked the white hair of his wife affectionately, and it seemed from Nimble Dick's manner he loved her and this affection of so many years was fondly returned. The Australian Blacks have unquestionably a great, deep affection for their relatives and old friends.

'I suppose not many Blackfellows could lie still for as long as I did, stretched out on the bough of a huge tree, watching hundreds of tribesmen looking for him. Many were sharp trackers. They could run the trail of a wallaby over miles of rocks. They could almost show you the place where a bird had flown through the air! I could see there were a lot of the clever fellows among them and I thought I could not be saved. If they killed me and did not find Lananglie, what could she do, poor thing, without someone to help her?

'The Pelicans looked up the trees, even climbed into some. One tribesman was so close that for a while I could have touched him with the end of my spear. They stopped close all day and camped there the night. They were all asleep when I slipped down the tree. I crawled all the way to Lananglie where she was nearly dead with cold and fright, still hidden in the hollow of the tree. We were hungry and thirsty. I took her in my arms and carried her away. Many times that night I thought she would die.

'We were a long way from the Pelicans by morning. We were at the foot of the ranges but it was not safe to stay there so we rested a while by a creek. I caught a possum and roasted him and the *lubra* ate some and said she was stronger. I rubbed the kidney fat of the Blacks we had killed on her back, arms and legs and after that she walked well. We went on up the mountains, walking in the creek so our tracks could not be seen. My *lubra* became too sick to walk anymore and I carried her. When the sun showed the middle of the day, we were in a very scrubby place and we lay down and slept. Then another thing happened that nearly killed us both.

'While we were asleep the clouds came up over the sky and made it dark like night. Rain fell and soon the flood came down the creek next to us but we were so tired and sleepy we didn't know until the water came all over us. It was so dark I thought it was the middle of the night. We stood up but nearly fell down again as the water was running very strong and almost carried us away. We nearly drowned. It was a long time before we could get out of the creek and onto the rocks. The thunder roared and the lightning struck trees close to us and the rain poured down hard.

'In the morning we ate the possum. I made the fire by rubbing grasstree, and we brought a fire stick with us, but now our fire was gone. Lananglie told me, 'I die before morning,' and she cried very much. So did I. Not for myself, but for the *lubra*. She was sick, cold and hungry. We thought how long that night was, but at last the thunder, lightning and rain left off and the clouds cleared away. It was nearly morning. Oh, I was glad.

'I found grass tree, but everything was so wet. I made a little flame but it fell on the damp ground and went out and many hours passed before I got fire. At last I had some stringy-bark in a blaze and we warmed ourselves. By then Lananglie was very sick, and there came pain into my heart. I killed a possum and two mopokes with my waddy and we had a feed. Then I made a gunyah of boughs and leaves and fern and in the morning Lananglie was a good deal better but we did not want to go on. We laughed a little that day because we thought the Pelican Blacks would never see our tracks after that rain.

'I hunted about and got plenty of tukka – birds and possums – and by the evening the *lubra* was feeling better. It made me glad to see her laugh as she used to before she was made ill by her cruel brother. We were happy, but I wondered where we could live for I knew we would be hunted, and that made me a bit sorry. The Pelicans went away but when they returned later to their camp the news of what happened came to our own people. They sent out men to look for us, so we went further into the mountains, Lananglie and I, to the places where the Blacks do not often go. We were very happy together.'

Nimble Dick and Lananglie left their tribe far behind them and lived in the mountains for about five years. By then, the elders would have forgiven them, as, on rare occasions, when a young man and woman did go away together, they were eventually permitted by the elders to return to their own people if it was believed they had been punished enough, and that it was clear the couple intended to remain together.

Any problems that Lananglie and Nimble Dick had with the Emus or the Pelicans were greatly reduced by the intrusion of white men and stock into their country.

Chapter Three

The First Shadow

The settler, in recording Nimble Dick's events of past years, said, 'It was remarked frequently by the Blacks that when they listen to us speaking they think we hiss. That is because, we imagine, of the frequent occurrence of the letters 'C' and 'S' in the English language.'

'I was a good big fellow when I first saw a white man. My word I was frightened! I ran away. So did all our people. We didn't stop either for a good while. We all said it was a devil. My blood was cold for many days. My brother was little when it happened and he could not speak. The fright made him dumb and he never did speak, though he lived till he had a long beard.

'Our tribe was very large and we could not stay long in the one place as there was not enough to eat, so after some days we would shift. After seeing the white devil, we kept as far from the place as we could. One day I was hunting with three other young men when we saw a worse sight, and it made us a great deal more afraid. We did not know what it was.

'It approached us through the bush and we sprang up into the trees and hid ourselves among the leaves. This thing passed along close underneath us. It had four legs, two arms and two heads. It came to the little creek and it parted in two. We saw it had two more legs. Both parts went to the water and drank. It was very frightful and I thought I would fall out of the tree. The parts came together again and went away. We stayed where we were until sundown, then all of us, except one, got down. We couldn't get that young fellow to come out of the tree. He stayed there for two days.

'If you saw that thing for the first time you'd be frightened too.

None of us had seen a man on a horse before. I laugh now, but I didn't then, not for a long time after. It caused trouble in the camp because the doctors said we lied about the whole business and wanted to know what we had done with the missing tribesman. They would not believe there could be a beast with so many arms, heads and legs that could part itself into two and join up again. We were ordered not to speak about it as we would frighten the women and the other young men and children.

'Our people asked about the young fellow and told us they believed we had quarreled with him and speared him. They were angry and took us before the old men who shook their heads and told us if he was alive we must bring him to the camp. It was late in the day and we were afraid to go, so we went a little way and slept that night in a scrubby place. We tried all the next day to get the young fellow to come down but he would not move or speak. Two of us went into the tree and tried to get him but he held on so hard we had to leave him for fear he would fall, and then our people would say we had killed him. He stopped in the tree all that night, and we lay under it. We didn't sleep much. We were afraid the beast would return.

'In the morning we roasted some possums and he was so hungry that when he smelt them he came down very cautiously and took some of the meat, but he did not stay to eat it – he started off like a kangaroo dog towards the camp and we ran as hard as we could after him. He spouted out all we had seen. The old men were very angry and said we should all be speared for telling lies and making him back us up. There was a great row in the camp and everyone talked and made a terrible noise.

'I stood silently looking at the fire and one of the men called me. I turned quickly to go to him where he was sitting on the ground, but what I saw gave me such a fright I could not move or speak. There were two of the beasts close behind the old man. They were so close, the horses' noses were almost touching the heads of two of the old men. I will never forget that scene. The people saw me staring and when they looked that way, they saw the beasts too. Some started to run away and when the white men got off their horses and offered bread to the old men, everyone ran as fast as they could, the women and pickaninnies, and the men. Only one old man rose up and took his spear and faced the white men.

'He was a brave old man. I stopped there with him, but it was from fear. I thought the blood in my veins would never get warm again and the marrow in my bones was cold. The old man raised his spear, but his arm was stiff; he could not throw it. That was a good thing. The white men had guns and pistols. They would have shot him. I thought they were devils and was glad the old man did not throw it. At last he dropped the point and leaned on the spear. All this time the white men were talking. It sounded like hissing. The white men all hiss a good deal when they speak.

'They stayed some time, I cannot tell how long. They offered the old man a knife and when he would not take it they put it on the ground at his feet. They pointed to the west and hissed, and at last got on the horses and rode away. When they were out of sight, the old man turned round and saw all the people were gone but me. He muttered something about cowards and dropped to the ground and in a minute he was asleep. I thought he was dying. The sweat poured out of his body everywhere in great drops and he was quite cold. I knelt beside him. His limbs were shivering. I cried over him for he was a good old man.

'When he fell down, the knife was under his head. I was afraid to touch it because I thought it was cursed and was killing him, so I tried to get the old man's spear to move it, but he held it too tightly. I went to my own camp and got one of my spears. When I moved the knife I found the white men had left it open and the blade was sharp and in moving it, it cut the old man's forehead. A lot of blood came and that frightened me more. But I believe it did the old man good. He opened his eyes and sat up but when he saw the blood he was afraid. I tried to stop the bleeding but couldn't.

'The old man cried, and he told me many things to do when he was dead, and made me promise not to leave him. In a while he got better and stood up and the bleeding stopped. He said we had better leave and we took our spears and walked slowly away from the camp. We followed the tracks of our people and we found them just before dark, in a narrow gully in the ranges. They were surprised to see us as they thought the devils had killed us both. We told them they had not hurt us, only hissed a lot.

'We kept small fires going that night and the doctors and some of the old men kept by themselves. They worked hard all night, in the way that they know, to keep devils out of the camp.

'We stayed in scrubby places in the ranges for a long time. One day when I was out after possums I was so busy looking at a tree for tracks that I did not hear my cousin, Toolambel, come up behind me. When I turned round, he looked more like a devil than a Blackfellow. He was tired and in great fear. He belonged to a group of my tribe we hadn't seen for a long time, and was the son of my father's brother.

'Toolambel had been hunting and the same beasts we saw came close to him and when he ran away they followed him, but he got amongst rocks and scrub and hid. When they left he ran towards the ranges. He was afraid they would kill all his people. I took him to our camp and his story made all our people frightened again. He was a brave tribesman but we are all afraid of devils and no-one knew then that these white men and horses were not devils. After some time, more Blacks came to the ranges and said they had seen these things too.

'Some very wise old men came to the camp and they talked together for a long time. Then they told us that what we thought were white devils were the people without color. Their fathers had told them the devil put these people in darkness in the old time and they said they would come back some day. The old men could tell us nothing about the horses.

'We heard more white men were seen who had made huts and yards down to the west. Many Blacks came to the mountains and told us about sheep, bullock and horses, and how they all ate grass. They told us these animals ran away from the tribesmen. The old men and doctors talked a lot.

“Some of you must go to the west and watch them. Who will go?”

‘Toolambel was the first to call his name, and then I said I would go with him, then three more young tribesmen agreed to go with us.

‘“You remember that thing you told me of that made the old man’s head bleed?” Toolambel said to me. “We must get it before we go. If these things are men like us, that will make them bleed too.”

‘I did not want to look for it but we did. It was rusty – not bright as it was when the white men left it for the old man. Toolambel looked at it for a long time before he picked it up. We returned to the camp and showed it to the doctors and after a while they were not afraid of the knife.’

Chapter Four

More than a War

Since 1788, acts of violence – real and imagined – by the tribal people of Australia against the occupiers of the acquired Aboriginal territories, have been highlighted. Very rarely, until lately, was mention made of the atrocities committed against the Aborigines by white men who took over the country. More often the truth was withheld that many of the tribes were friendly, at first. Their attitude changed when they found the newcomers had not come in friendship. They had come to stay; to take their land; their food; their water; their labour and their lives.

Who better to tell the truth than Nimble Dick.

'We went down to the west and after many days we went near the white men. We got to be good friends with them and they gave us mutton and tea, knives and tomahawks. Some of us went back to our people and told them all about it. A lot of them came down to where we were on the station.

'Toolambel and I got to be shepherds and we prided ourselves very much on keeping the sheep in good condition. When we went to the station first there were two masters and they were always very good to us, giving food to the old people and the women and pickaninnies. They went away and left the overseer there to be master. He was a very sulky man and often swore at us and he would not give the old people and the women and pickaninnies anything to eat so they had to leave us and they went away to live in the old places. The trouble was thousands of sheep were there and they soon drove the kangaroos and emus off and ruined the watering places.

'The tribe soon found the times were not so good for us as they were before the white men came and this made the old men unhappy and they grumbled a good deal. I believe they did think sometimes, whether there was not some plan to be made that would drive them away. Blackfellows don't like to starve and you can't blame the old men for growling. Ours was a fine hunting country before it was stocked with cattle and sheep. We had never been hungry, except that time we hid in the ranges from the white fellows because we thought them to be devils.

'Instead of hunting first, then resting, the young tribesmen had the hard work of keeping the old men, the women and children in food. Some of the old men got sick and they died. That made the young tribesmen feel worse in their minds about the white men and they said, 'These are not the good people without color that were to come. They are the devils we thought they were at first.'

'One day a wild dog got among Toolambel's flock and killed many and scattered the rest all over the country. When the overseer knew about that poor fellow Toolambel's accident with the sheep, he came with two men and tied him to a tree. The overseer flogged him with the stock-whip until his back was raw. He rubbed turpentine all over it and Toolambel nearly died.

'I had hard work to get him back to the tribe because he was in such pain and so weak. When our people saw this cruel thing, they were in a great fury. The old men said the tribe had to be mustered and the tribesmen must go and kill the white men. Messengers were sent all over our own country and into the country of the next tribe, and the men soon gathered. We made the camp in the scrubby ranges out of the way of the whites.

'When one of the parties belonging to the tribal land next to ours got the message to come to our camp, they left their sick people in camp with some old men and three children. While the tribesmen were making their way to us they found a stray sheep. They killed it and ate it. The next day the overseer found the sheep bones lying round the camp fires. He went back to the station and sent word to another station overseer to send some men to him. He was with his own men and the others when they went on horse-back with guns and pistols and came to the camp where the sick women were with the old men and the children.

They shot them all.

'When the tribes people found out they would not be quiet any longer. They were mad. Some of them went down to an outstation in the night, with Toolambel at the head of them. I did not go that time. They killed two shepherds but the hut-keeper got away and went to the home station. Our tribes people drove the sheep away. The next day the overseer and a lot of his men came out and followed the tracks to where the sheep were. A good many young Blackfellows – good fighting men – had stayed with the sheep and when the whites rode up, they did not run away. They had good spears, many of them were new ones, and they threw them at the overseer and his stockmen. One of the men was speared in the shoulder and two horses were hurt. The white men fired their guns and some tribesmen were killed. It was a big fight but so many of the warriors got killed and hurt, that at last those that were left ran from the place.

'When the news came to the camp, we all took up our spears. There were many of us and we were not afraid. We were cranky, wanting to kill the white men. Toolambel was brought back to the camp with a broken arm and when we heard his groans and the moans of some of the men who had the balls from the white men's weapons in their bodies, we shouted out that we would kill our enemies. The women raised their voices in great sorrow while the old men cried out we must kill the white men.

'It was moonlight when we started. We knew the stockmen would take the sheep back to the station run, and that meant they would camp on the road. We agreed to surround them and spear them all at daylight. There were a lot of us with hundreds of new spears. We walked very fast until we saw their fires and could see they were camped by a large waterhole. We lay down and talked about what to do next. We sent some young fellows to steal up close to the camp and see how many men were there and then to take the hobbles off the horses.

'They crept up to the camp but found the horses were tied close to the fires so they had to leave them. There were four men there but the overseer was not with them. One of the warriors who had been in the fight that morning yelled out with rage when he heard that, and we had to hold him and keep him quiet in case the whites heard him. One of the tribesmen howled out like a wild dog to trick the whites – and they fired off their guns to frighten the dog away. We lay still making our plans until the rays of morning made the first light into the sky and we were glad. We seemed to have waited so long for the attack. We do not like to meet our enemies in the night. We stole away under the shadow of the trees and silently surrounded the men and sheep in a large circle.

'Two men were still asleep, one was cooking breakfast and another was leading his horse round the sheep, letting him feed. When our leader threw a fire-stick in the air we answered the signal and rushed down to the camp. The whites had no time to get their guns as the mob of Blackfellows, mad for their blood, rushed down on them, yelling and shrieking and throwing spears. The only one to escape us was the shepherd. As soon as he saw the fire-stick he jumped on his horse and galloped away and never stopped to help the others. He did not cry out to them to give them any warning and I thought he was a great coward. Many spears were thrown at him but he was not struck. We left the dead men but took away their guns and pistols and the powder and balls and caps. Some of us knew how to load them because we had seen it done at the sheep station.

'We drove the sheep back towards the ranges again as fast as we could because we knew the white men would soon be after us. We wanted to get into a steep part where horses could not get and by the afternoon we were at the foot of the ranges. It was hot and the sheep were too tired to go any further. We said, 'Never mind, we have the guns. We will shoot the devils when they find us.' I said, 'Let us load them,' but the men who had carried them said they had already done that. They knew nothing about it and had rammed the balls into the muzzles, and no powder. They were of no use to us. I told the warriors the guns would not go off because they should have put in the powder and they were very surprised and sorry. We tried to get the balls out but couldn't. When evening came, we drove the sheep into a very steep place in the ranges and made bough yards for them. The tribesmen broke one leg of every sheep so they could not run away.

'The white men had not followed us as we expected and we learnt afterwards that the shepherd who had left his friends to be killed without trying to fire at the Blacks, got so frightened he lost himself getting back to the home-station. He didn't arrive there until the middle of the night so the overseer knew nothing about what we had done. He thought the sheep were safe with his four men on their way to the out-station.

'In the morning when there were no signs of the white men, a lot of us went out in small groups to look for them. If we saw them, we were to trick them by running in different directions away from where the sheep were yarded and make great smokes to lead them to the wrong place. In the afternoon, my Uncle Billy and a little fellow called Tommy Blue, were down on the creek when they saw some white men coming. They led them a pretty dance until it was getting dark. I suppose they were frightened to camp out that night and Uncle Billy and Tommy watched them turn back.

'After that, the whites got five or six policemen to help them and a good many times they fired at some of the warriors but they could not hit them, or catch them but they galloped about very hard firing off a terrible lot of powder and ball.

As there was no water where we had the sheep, we camped in a gully a little way off where the old men, women and children who had come with us stayed all the time. We didn't let the sheep out of the bough and brush yards we made. They couldn't walk with a broken leg and many of them died. We had good feasts during that time and some of the old women nearly killed themselves with eating too much mutton!

'We thought the whites would never find us and I don't think they would have for a long time only that one day they caught a young Blackfellow and put handcuffs on him. They give him nothing to eat or drink and said they would shoot him if he didn't show them where the sheep were hidden. At last he was forced to do as they wanted.

'There were a lot of us at the yards asleep after feasting all night. Early in the morning I saw the men and troopers coming and I called our fellows. Some woke, jumped up, and got their spears. We stood behind the high brush fence and threw them when the whites came up the stony hill. Their horses had a hard work picking their way. None of our spears hit the men but they immediately fired at us and the balls came cutting through the fence. Five of our warriors dropped to the ground, dead, or wounded. By this time the rest of the men were well awake and we gave the whites another shower of spears and three were hit. One horse fell, speared in the belly. Because our spears were not jagged, but all made of reeds with small wooden heads, the men were able to pull them out of each other.

'Bang, bang, bang, came another lot of balls and so more of the warriors bodies were stretched out on the ground. I can't forget that fight. I slipped about in blood. It was all over my feet. The poor fellows that were down and not dead groaned and cried. Uncle Billy was shot through the chest. I think the ball went right through him. He was lying close to me. 'I am going to die' he told me. 'Give me a leg of sheep,' and I gave it to him. He ate it till he was quite dead and it seemed to do him good. I don't think he felt the pain so much, but he did bleed a lot.

'The whites kept coming nearer and we threw more spears. One struck the overseer in his shoulder and he fell off his horse. Two of our young men ran out to waddy him but they were shot dead before they could get at him. The rest of the whites rode up quite close to us and kept firing amongst us. We fought hard but so many of us were shot that we at last had to run. Several balls passed so close to my head I could hear them whistle along. We ran away from the main camp because we thought the whites would follow us and murder the old men women and children. But they did find them.

'We returned to the camp in the evening and it was a sad thing to see. There were only three of four people left alive, even though the troopers had cut them with their swords. They had killed all the lubras and pickanninies they could find. Some got away and hid, and we never saw them again for a long time I think forty or fifty of our people were killed. My own father and mother were shot dead and their bodies were wounded all over with swords cuts.

'We knew the white men and the troopers were down at the sheep yards. They had fires going and their dogs barked. We could not stay at our camp and our hearts were troubled with grief. We took away those of our people who were alive and left the dead. We cursed all the white men. We lived in misery and fear as we took the sick people further from the death camp, day after day. We knew our spears were no good against the guns and pistol and every day we went further. We did not want to see white men any more. Our tribe was in great sorrow.

'As time went by more white men came into our country with their sheep and cattle and we had to go among them. I never stole anymore from them, but some of our people did and many were shot. I told you my own Lananglie has been shot twice.

'Before the white men came there were hundreds of Blackfellow in my country. How many now? They are nearly all gone. This is what makes me wake up and cry often when I lay my heard on my breast at the campfire at night.'

It has been recorded by the first squatters that some of the Aborigines looked older than their years because of the deprivations they suffered after the coming of the white races to their territories.

Chapter Five

Occupation and Contact 1837–1850s

After repeated reports reached London of the ill-treatment dealt out to the Aborigines of New South Wales, a Protectorate was appointed for the Port Phillip District in 1837. This consisted of a Chief Protector and four assistants, and by 1839 they were based in Geelong, the Mornington Peninsula, and the Goulburn and Loddon areas. By then the landholders realized running their stations with Aboriginal labour was a quick and efficient way to success and wealth. The Protectorate operated until 1850, but during that time most of the squatters refused to co-operate with the Protectors. Aboriginal deaths increased and the Government discussed the cost of a Protection scheme.

The tribal people of the Murray Valley had their favourite camping sites and where-ever the waterways flowed or trickled, lay in lagoons, swept along in rivers, dawdled in creeks, wandered through valleys of billabongs, swamps, marshes and distributaries, there were the families. Descendants tell of the sacredness of 'the Old People's totems' and how, as very young children, this awareness was passed to them. There was food in abundance and they lived on nature's supply of wild fruits and berries, root, vegetation, fish, water and land birds and animals. At night everyone enjoyed watching the young men prepare their frail-looking bark canoes for fishing on the Murray. They placed a pile of earth in the centre for ballast, and a mound of clay close to it on which a small fire was set, and as it burned the light attracted the fish making them easy targets for spears.

The Yotti Yotta had plenty of food in the great red gum and box forests on both sides of the Murray. A seemingly never ending supply of food roamed, swam and waded throughout an area they called 'paama,' the word they used to describe the existence in great numbers of the insect-eating plover. Here the lakes, swamps and lagoons were havens for fish, swans, ducks and ibis, and the tall trees rang with the calls of thousands of birds whose eggs were a special delicacy. If all that was not enough the river people still had the emus, echidnas, kangaroos and possums.

Legends are told by the descendants of the Yotti Yotta in which floods changed the course of the Murray many years ago. The tribes people saw the rushing waters burst the banks and roar across new ground, swamping the small trees until it reached the Barmah (paama) Only the tops of the tallest trees were visible. Today this forest is the largest of the Victorian river red gum forests where approximately 24,600 ha of red gum and 700 ha of box forest grow. Within the forest area there are about 3,000 ha of swamps, grasslands and lakes. It is the red gum Eucalyptus Camaldulensis that survives the floods to reach maturity in the Barmah State Forest.

When white men came into the Murray Valley country by every available means, the tribal culture began to shatter immediately because the whole life system of the Aborigines was based on the very environment in which they lived. Every plant, root, tree, animal, bird, fish river, lagoon, creek, hill, hollow or mountain, cave or flat rock surface, sand hill, in fact everything on the earth and above held some significance. The sacred places for initiation ceremonies, the burial places, carved trees, the cooking areas, now called middens, sand drawings, tool and weapon exchange boundaries as well as tribal boundaries, were all part of the communal life of sharing.

Ceremonial stones so reverently placed in wide circles were soon kicked and knocked out of the way by stock and farming implements. The Yotti Yotta groups were broken and scattered, often into Baraparapa or Jeithi land and as the white men took up the country the aborigines moved from station to station searching for a spot to put up a mia-mia hoping the squatter would give them food to replace the loss of their native animals and vegetation. Many of the first wave of squatters and their convict stockmen were cruel and thoughtless in their dealings with the tribes people.

The Blacks should be kindly treated as they are of great service in stripping bark, showing new runs, tracking lost sheep. Moreover kind treatment will be found the great secret of restraining their tendency to furtive and vindictive depredations. At the same time, with kindness must be mingled a manifestation of the most perfect fearlessness, but it should not be mere parade and bravado. They are quick at detecting the true feeling that dictates an action. Arms should always be ready, and securely kept, and they should know it too.[1]

When however, due to the trickery, lies cruelty and dishonest dealings of white men, the Aborigines struck back in their own defence, publicity was given to their 'depredations.' A tribeswoman on the Murray named Niniginna was burnt severely when a hutkeeper threw hot fat from his frying pan over her. The men of her tribe could have paid back her attacker but no one would have known the reason and this would have been described as another native depredation. Such cases as this did occur.[2]

Native food disappeared quickly as kangaroo hunts became sport for white men and women such as the one described in the Riverine Herald near the residence of Mr Thomas Robertson. There were about twenty equestrians present among whom were two ladies. The hunt is spoken of as the most exciting that had taken place on the Campaspe for many years. The animals were chased for some twenty miles to Paboinboolook, now known as Lake Cooper. Kangaroo hunts featured on most of the station properties in order that the pastures and grass were reserved for stock. As the native game of all sorts decreased the cattle and sheep stealing episodes by the tribesmen became more frequent and so did the deaths of their people as the thefts were brutally revenged.[3]

The Gnurellean group who spoke the Yotti Yotta language lived mainly in the Gunbower area and they would have known about the slaughter of some of their neighbours, the Baraparapa, near the Wakool River on the New South Wales side of the Murray. Cattle stealing was the reason given by the white men when they organized a Black Hunt along the Wakool. They found their quarry and their beef. The Baraparapa men were sitting round a pile of meat, all cut and ready to go on the fire. The hunters opened fire. The men grabbed their spears and tomahawks and fought for their lives but the odds were too great, and those who could run did so leaving their dead and wounded. The white men were quite satisfied with their days work. The result of their victory tended to subdue and quiet the Blacks for some time, giving them an example of the efficacy of the white fellows' weapon, the musket.[4]

The occupation of New South Wales was responsible for diseases previously unknown to the country. Before the Murray Valley was stocked the Aboriginal tribes had already been affected by smallpox which they call thinba mika. A Pelican tribesman named Nankero was badly marked but he was one of the luckier ones who had survived an epidemic. He believed the disease had come down the Murray River infecting the tribes along the way. Early settlers were told by the aborigines many children died from thinba mika, and women and men. Nankero said when they became too ill to walk some could manage to crawl to the river to drink, and they would die there.[5]

It is estimated that in 1834 the Aborigines numbered 17,000 in Port Phillip (Victoria). In 1839 there were 5,822 white people and the following year this increased to 10,291. The Aboriginal population crashed as quickly as the numbers escalated on the census lists for the white newcomers.[6]

Overlanders established stock runs along the rivers and clashes with tribesmen were consistently reported to the Superintendent of Port Phillip, Charles Joseph La Trobe. Mounted police were dispatched to the trouble spots, and the Goulburn, Campaspe and Murray tribes earned the distinction of being referred to as violent.

The overlanders lost no time in telling the new chums, recent arrivals in the colony, the bloodthirsty stories about the natives. One of these men was Captain Charles Hutton. He set up his run on the Campaspe of 144,900 acres adjoining Heathcote, and called it Campaspe Plains. His station was in the country of the

Pinpandoor and although he had enough land to keep his stock fit he resented the 'intrusion' of the tribespeople on his run. It was not long before the mounted police and a band of white men, were intent on clearing the Pinpandoor and their neighbours, the Yotti Yotta, from Campaspe Plains.

The mounted men caught up with the tribesmen at the junction of the Campaspe and opened fire on them, shooting indiscriminately. Several of the hunters declared they killed five or six but the Aboriginal Protector disagreed and said a great number were slain.[7]

By 1843 there were 8,211 white women living in Port Phillip but not enough to gratify the sexual cravings of the 24,103 white men. The native women were easy prey, and no questions asked. Many of the so called skirmishes between the tribesmen and the whites were caused by the kidnapping, rape, torture and killing of tribal women by white settlers.

There is no question that this accusation is correct. It is untrue to make the excuse these attacks were made only by the convict and exconvicts, the 'lower class' white men. 'Respected gentlemen' such as doctors, station owners, sons of politicians, hotel keepers etc. were equally guilty.

In the February of 1843 La Trobe wrote of a skirmish at Curr's property at the junction of the Murray and the Goulburn rivers. A Bangerang tribesman was captured but La Trobe had him discharged as he was ignorant of the character of the proceedings instigated against him.[8] Twenty-two year old Edward Curr said the tribesman lived on the traditional land which he had taken possession of in 1842 for his father.[9]

Curr managed various stations for his father for ten years including Wolfscrag near Heathcote, Corop and Caragar near Rochester, Colbibabbin near Lake Cooper, Tongala on the Goulburn east of Echuca and Moira on the Murray and Goulburn rivers, later known as Upper and Lower Moira. He was one of the first squatters to form stock runs in these areas and was aware of the original owners and their culture very early in his career. His limited choice of servants were mostly old gaol-birds and expiree convicts who were independent, rowdy men and came from the ranks of horse-stealers, killers, drunken and disorderly soldiers and marines.[10]

While at Wolfscrag in 1841 natives attacked his neighbour ten miles off and were accused of killing some of his men. When the Chief Protector of Aborigines, George Robinson, investigated the report he discovered the natives had earlier been mistreated by the white men. Even so six soldiers were sent from Melbourne to protect this particular squatter.

One of the mounted police told Curr the Aborigines had committed depredations down on the McIvor Creek and warned him to be on guard as they would kill him if they saw he was unarmed in revenge for some of their people who had been shot fifteen miles away on the banks of the Campaspe. Some days later Curr was confronted by four naked tribesmen, their ribs painted like those of a skeleton and white circles round their eyes. They stood quietly, spears in their hands, and in understandable English they threatened to spear him. Curr replied he would shoot them and they gathered their possum rugs from the bushes and left. In later years he recorded he had not killed any Aborigines.

Curr's application to the Government for fifty square miles of land near the Murray, twenty-five on each side of the Goulburn near Echuca. He named the run Tongala although that was the name for the Murray river used by the Aborigines of the Goulburn. Before he occupied the run he was given many accounts of battles between the tribesmen and the whites by a stockman from the Wyuna Station, Curr's easterly neighbor.

He was not surprised when he found a wounded Bangerang man bleeding from his face and his possum rug had blood on it from his arm. He could not speak or understand English. When he was on the Wyuna cattle station that morning the hut-keeper ordered him away and when Nosie, as he was dubbed by stockmen, made no move he was shot in the arm and another shot was so close it tore away part of his beard. After tending to the wound Curr rode to Wyuna to confront the hut keeper who told him he would shoot as many of them who come there when he was alone.

When shearing time came around at Tongala, Curr left his overseer in charge assisted by some of the Bangerang men who, he said, had begun to make themselves useful about the place. Later when the Border Police were on patrol around Tongala the news reached Curr of seventy tribesmen having speared a sheep each on the Moira run. The police captured a tribesman and padlocked him to the kitchen wall slabs and next morning took their captive away from the station, determined he should lead them to his tribe but he managed to escape and headed for the river. The police shot him before he reached the water. They loaded his body into a canoe and Curr declared the current conveyed its ghastly freight down the stream.

Soon after, one of the shepherds carelessly allowed 120 lambs to wander off from his fold and the Aborigines rounded them up and feasted on lamb chops for days. The police arrived to disrupt the happy scene but the natives escaped to the other side of the river. One tribesman stopped long enough to hurl his spear across the water into the arm of a policeman. Back at the camp the police found Warri and his wife Mirandola. They allowed her to leave but Warri was roped round his neck and forced to walk to Tongala behind a mounted policeman's horse. He was taken to the Melbourne gaol where, three months later, Curr visited him in his cell. He was ill, depressed, and expecting to be hung. Curr arranged for his release and two weeks later Warri was back with Mirandola in his own country at Tongala. He was forever Curr's friend for having saved his life.

The mounted police shot tribes people who had nothing to do with causing the squatters any loss of stock and it was then a case of mistaken identity. They were a frightening sight dressed in uniform and carrying cavalry sabres and carbines. They would appear before a group suspected of stealing and then at a gallop, sabres in hand, the troopers industriously loaded and discharged their cabines. Some of the settlers believed less evidence was needed to destroy a tribe than to send an habitual drunkard to the lockup for a few hours.

When the Protectorate was terminated one man continued working officially as the Guardian of Aborigines named William

Thomas. A number of tribal men were persuaded to join the mounted police. He knew Reverend John Merewether when in the 1850s he was attending to his congregation in the Murray River district. He noted the tribesmen 'shoot we'll, ride well, make excellent mounted police, are very honest, not addicted to pilfering, great newsmongers, wonderful mimics, and pick up our language very rapidly.' In spite of that, alcohol was given in payment for their work on many stations.[11]

Merewether found they were badly treated by the squatters and also the shepherds and stockmen who lived miles away from the main station houses. Merewether heard the common statement amongst bushmen 'that it is no use to hit a blackfellow with your fist, he won't feel it' and the nearest instrument was used for punishment.[12]

He was disgusted with the conditions under which some of the native people lived. In many places he found the elderly and sick were dying from lack of food and medical attention. Common killers which left children orphans or wiped out whole families were mumps and measles. Venereal disease had been spread amongst the tribes by white men.

Merewether's temporary residence was on the property called Moolpa southeast of Balranald which Dr George Mein and his brother, Pulteney, occupied during the 1850s. They held thousands of acres in the vicinity of Moulamein and the rivers Edward, Murray, Wakool and Murrumbidgee. The station was on the north bank of the Edward River and on the edge of a plain which extended to the Murrumbidgee. There were up to sixty tribespeople camped not far from the station house.

Merewether wrote '… these poor people pick up what they can get and make themselves useful in many ways.' They had not become regular workers for the squatters and tried to hang on to the remnants of their tribal lives, without much success. Most of the shepherds and hut keepers on the plains were old convicts from Sydney and most had one disease or another. They were stationed about twenty miles from the head station often in the areas visited by the tribespeople.

Within two years of Merewether's visit to Moolpa many of the Aborigines he met now worked for the squatters across their own countries.

Chapter Six

The Meeting of the Waters 1850s–1863

The peninsula formed by the Campaspe River flowing into the Murray was surveyed by Philip Chauncy in 1854. The Yotti Yotta described the area to him in one word, 'echuca,' which meant the meeting of the waters. He gave their title to the area, Echuca.

The group of clan members of the Yotti Yotta, with their own distinct names who managed to live through the droughts, floods, white occupation and diseases, used their old methods of food gathering and cooking whenever they could, and their culture survived in the same manner. A new born baby always received a great amount of love and attention. Reverend John Bulmer of Gippsland wrote, 'On the Murray it was, after a day or two, smeared all over with charcoal and grease as it's young skin had not got that hue which it would have after exposure to the sun. In the meantime it must not look too white so something temporary must be done with charcoal to give it the proper colour. It was always carefully tended by it's parents.'[1]

The unwanted rumours and reports of gold discoveries in Victoria were accepted by the Government and by 1853 the colony was teeming with diggers. They noticed the camps of the Aborigines near the rivers as they went from one goldfield to another and wondered how much protection from sun or rain the families could expect under the bough, bark and branch mia-mias. They knew when they had to erect the shelters for themselves.

In 1853 the tribal people saw for the first time two wooden paddle steamers on the Murray River. The flourishing goldfields around the Goulburn area caused a South Australian man named William Randell to believe a trade steamer could not fail to be a success. With the help of his brother he built the paddle steamer *Mary Ann* of red gum.[2]

Philip La Mothe Snell Chauncy. (Courtesy of Miss Winifred Chauncy.)

Philip Chauncy was born in England in 1816 and came to Australia in 1839. Two years later, twenty-five years of age, he was appointed Assistant Government Surveyor in Western Australia (Swan River Colony). In 1853 he had his wife and children moved to Victoria where he was appointed Government Assistant Surveyor at McIvor. One of the important aspects of Philip's Chauncy's career relates to his consistent interest and concern for the original occupiers of the lands he surveyed. This included the area he named Echuca, the word used by the tribal people in describing the land Chauncy had chosen. He also surveyed further areas including the country at Dunolly, Castlemaine and Ballarat. His communication with the Aboriginal people and documentation of events earned Philip La Mothe Snell Chauncy, as he signed his name, the title of Anthropologist.

The second vessel was the *Lady August* which Francis Cadell had built for him in Sydney. He challenged Randell to a race which lasted two days. Randell achieved the honour of being the first white man to navigate the Murray. Cadell's crew included three Aborigines, two South Sea Islanders, one Chinese and two Indians.[3] He was known to kidnap Islanders and ship them to wealthy land owners and plantation managers and was one of many sea captains to be called 'a black birder.'

The Murray River trade began from the day in August 1853 when Randell pulled his paddle-steamer into the riverbank at

Maiden's Punt, now Moama, where exconvict, James Maiden had begun operating his own punt and ferry seven years earlier.

By 1857 the river trade had exploded to such an extent that ten steamers worked the water and passenger steamers followed, including Cadell's.[4] On one of his trips he had the Governor of South Australia on board and, wishing to make a good impression, he decided to introduce him to a head tribesman. He chose a tribal doctor who was well-known along the rivers by his white name of Mr McGregor. (Peter McGregor owned Minindie Station on the Darling.) Cadell explained to the the tribesman that the great Governor was a man who had power and held high office in the white man's world. To make sure the doctor knew he was to meet a man of some prominence Cadell impressed on him he was a big man. It was a fact the Governor was a tall and well built man. When Cadell introduced the famous doctor to the Governor he marched straight up to him and poked, prodded and patted him on is ample stomach and said, 'No gammon. You big fellow.'[5]

Tribal doctors were respected for their power and held in awe by their people although they had no authority regarding the affairs of the group. John Atkinson, who can trace his family back to the 1800's, said, 'the controlling people in our tribes were the elders and they handled everything, health, education and government.[6] When a council was held all the men were permitted to speak, holding a club or boomerang in his hand. The young men listened to their elders and their advice was followed.'[7]

Around the area of Chauncy's 'meeting of the waters'[8] a licence for land was taken up by Irishmen Hugh and Robert Glass in 1557 and became known as Wharparella Station (Wharparilla). Consisting of 76,000 acres on the Murray and Campaspe rivers adjoining Echuca, this was the country of the Wollithiga families of the Yotti Yotta. Their word for water was wolla and sections of their land were, and are, subject to flooding. The Glass brothers could, if they wished, run 12,000 sheep on Wollithiga ground.[9] Five years later Hugh Glass held forty-nine runs and was the wealthiest man in Victoria. He was another ‘big man’ in the white community of Victoria but the natives on some of his holdings died of starvation and disease.

It is necessary to know a little about Hugh Glass as he was one of the most successful landgrabbers in the State, either legally or through the trickery of land-law loopholes. He immigrated in 1840 when he was twenty-three years of age and began his notorious climb to fame, wealth and power as a farmer, then storekeeper. He became a partner of (Sir) William F. Stawell as a station agent, and from that time he was on the top rung of success.

John (Sandy) Atkinson, 1980. A respected and well-known elder.

He was ruthless in his business activities and, at times, was accused of corruption. He built an expensive home in Melbourne, Flemington House, (which is still standing), and men and women of culture were drawn to his side, visiting him and enjoying the pleasures he supplied. Excellent food and drink, inspections of his aviaries of beautiful birds, tanks full of fish, and artificial lakes complete with swans. The drought of 1865 and the fall in wool prices were instrumental in the downfall of Hugh Glass. Accused of bribery, he spent several days in gaol. In May 1871, he took his own life.

Plans for the much talked about Iron Bridge over the Murray connecting Echuca and Moama were underway and the arguments surrounding the project rivaled the accounts in the *Riverine Herald* of the adventures of the celebrated bushranger, Daniel Morgan, and other outlaws who helped themselves to anyone's property. Robbery under arms kept the backwoods settlers on the alert.

The townspeople had their problems too, as men and women were constantly charged with drunkenness, or annoying the good people of Echuca by riding horses on the paths, being violent, breaking windows and banging kerosene tins to make a hideous din. The press revealed two men were in such a state of intoxication while driving their dray that one fell out and the wheel ran over his head. When they were found by a settler, the driver of the vehicle was still too intoxicated to render assistance to his partner.

The daring actions of a gang of men on the tramp up-country scandalized Echuca's community as they feared the men set a bad example to the younger generation. The tramps had the nerve to take King Henry Hopwood's ferry to cross the river then left it to drift away.

Canoe Tree's survival on former Glass Property, Wharparella Station, 1980. (Courtesy Jack O'Mullane.)

The paddle steamers continued to collect bales of wool and sheep skins from the stations along the river and with the busy trade came a number of accidents. In December 1863 Captain William Randell, in the *Bunyip* with twenty-two passengers on board and towing two barges loaded with wool, was faced with the outbreak of a fire. He remained at the wheel until he had to jump overboard through flames. Four people were killed and the paddle steamer and cargo were lost.[10]

During the 1860s the Selection Acts were passed with the intention of opening up the country and prizing from the squatters some of the Crown Land held by them on lease. Arguments, fights and threats broke out between selectors and squatters, and while white men wrangled over who would own the land, the tribal people became fewer in number. They still caught *yabba,* the Murray crayfish, and *woneg,* the eel, and they ate *cumbunya*, the root of the common reed, with their fish.[11]

The native food sources were now restricted and areas where good food was obtainable were quickly snatched up by the landowners. For instance, Moira Lake had sustained generations of the Yotti Yotta but by 1863 a prosperous fishing company had control of the water and everything in it. The company coach was loaded twice weekly with the fish and sent to Echuca to be off-loaded onto the *Lady Augusta,* the *Wakool,* and other trading steamers. An occasional warning was issued about the quantity being taken from the lake especially when the river was low and fish were scarce.[12]

The leeches were also harvested and sold to the medical profession locally as well as being exported to England. They brought an excellent financial return. Nick Kelsall, who worked on the outrigger barges on the Murray during the 1930s recalled,

While rabbiting close to the Moira Lakes we watched two Aborigines we thought had gone mad. They were stirring up the mud from the bottom of the lake, then banging the top of the water with flat boards. When they came out they had two buckets full of leeches. What made them latch onto the board I've no idea, unless they thought they had a victim. This was a means of earning some money as the Melbourne hospitals paid well for these aquatic bloodsuckers.[13]

The Moira and Barmah Lakes and forest areas had the settlers' stock grazing where once the grey kangaroos and emus were supreme. While settlers steadfastly made inroads throughout Aboriginal territory some of the tribal families visited secluded spots for native food known only to themselves. On 30 December 1865 the *Riverine Herald* published the description of one such excursion made by an unnamed white man with a group of tribal men and women:

With a great deal of persuasion and a considerable donation in the shape of tobacco and sugar, besides a little money, I succeeded in securing a seat in one of the two canoes that were to start at daybreak the following morning for a lagoon some four miles down the river. The early start was made to avoid the mid-day heat which in this season of the year is almost intolerable, the thermometer not unfrequently standing at 112 in the shade.

The party consisted of four tribesmen, two lubras and myself, and as far as they were concerned, all in holiday attire. They had wallaby skins cut into thin strips tied tassel-wise and hung around the waist serving the double purpose of fig leaves or fly flappers as occasion required. Niger, the head man of his tribe, had by way of head dress, a kerchief of many colours bound turban style round his head. In this he had stuck a knife, a pipe and some tobacco. From his forehead dangled a bunch of kangaroo teeth which swung to and fro with every motion of the head. The group did not have any clothing. When ignorance is bliss 'tis folly to be wise, and the ignorance and innocence of these people makes their seeming want of propriety perfectly pardonable.

We flitted smoothly along on the broad shining bosom of the mighty river till we came to the place of rendezvous, a secluded oval-shaped sheet of water which was about a miles in circumference and shut in on all sides by gigantic trees whose huge white limbs twined and twisted into a sort of fantastic framework enclosing in security, the thousands of aquatic fowls that were resting on the smooth water. We landed at a small creek, now dry, guarded by enormous red gum trees, their majestic trunks standing firm and unflinching, their high heads covered with evergreen foliage mingling and intermixing thus forming an archway so grand that a man's puny efforts could never attain. Through this archway, almost dark from its density, the waters of the Murray found their way during the winter months to the lagoon.

We were no sooner on the sandy ground than Niger's quick eye detected three or four white cranes quietly feeding on the margin of the lagoon. As these birds are just as cautious as they are beautiful the greatest silence on our part was necessary. Once they are aware of danger they fly off uttering the most terrible screams and so disturbing all the game within hearing. This causes them to be the most disliked creature by all sportsmen, Aboriginal or otherwise.

Without as much as a twig cracking or a leaf rustling, a net made of the Murray rush, which was some ninety or one hundred yards square, was lifted from the canoe and spread carefully on the ground, then rolled up and carried across the mouth of the inlet. Niger and Mako then fixed the net between two trees, each taking a corner high up into the branches on either side of the water. The lubras were well hidden amongst the rushes and leaves, holding down the lower corners of the net.

Meantime Niger and Mako had gone stealthily along, one on each side of the lagoon. In their hands they held pieces of bark that were formed like hawks with outstretched wings. One of the men perched himself high in a tree about midway up the lagoon and the other did the same at the furthest point. All being ready, the deathlike stillness was pierced by a wild shrill whistle that seemed to make the very water shiver. At the same time, the bark hawks were thrown high in the air and came swooping down so like the birds of prey they were meant to look like, the game rose in the wildest confusion and fear.

At that moment the dainty white cranes flew screaming over the tree tops; the marsh hens, with tails erect made off to the nearest bushes for shelter but the poor stupid ducks, always flying along the water making for the river, made their mistake. In their blind haste they flew by the dozens into the outspread net. Their stiffened necks became entangled in the meshes and before they could free themselves the net dropped over them, and cleverly and quickly rolled up by the lubras stationed below.

Niger, Mako and the other two tribesmen, breathless with running, were soon on the spot. Upward of forty birds were netted; some of the black ducks weighing as much as six pounds; the teal, too, were fine. The nulla-nulla commenced its work. Some of the fattest were immediately thrown upon the fire with small regard to plucking or any other dressing, and when little more than warm through they were dispatched with great gusto. When this meal was finished the leftovers were stowed away on the canoes. The lubras were ordered to paddle back to the camp as the men intended to walk, that being much less trying than paddling the four miles against the stream. I also preferred walking, not caring to sit for three or four hours breathing in the stale odour of fish oil which the young women had anointed themselves with from head to foot.

Oil and grease from fish and animals were used by the Aborigines often as a protection from mosquito and fly attack. Their bodies were also smeared with these substances for tribal and medical reasons.

The Wongatpan group had their main camp at the junction of the Murray and Broken Creek, Baala, about four miles upriver from Barmah in a small part of the Moira country they called wongat. They lived chiefly on roots of vegetation and fish, and rarely left the waterways and reed beds of the Murray. They used nets and short barbed spears to catch the fish and waterfowl. This group rubbed fish oil on their bodies.

Graziers and farmers experimented with growing tobacco, cotton and oranges in the Murray Valley and Hugh Glass, with his overseer and station hands at Wharparella Station, was applauded for his success with orange growing.[14]

Another identity who claimed to be the King and founder of Echuca was the ex-convict who made good, and jocosely referred to by the residents as King Henry Hopwood. He had ten acres of grapes growing well and brought the judgment that 'this must be a forerunner of a vine growing district.' He had earned himself a niche in history as he already had his pontoon bridge over the Murray and a span across the Campaspe which was just as well, for in the September of 1863 the waters of the Campaspe flooded into the Echuca township.[15]

Hopwood confidently advertised his Echuca Bridge Hotel in less than twenty words: 'As this is already known to be the best Hotel out of Melbourne further comment is unnecessary.'

The keepers of most of the hotels, grog shanties and inns accepted the money for alcohol by Aboriginal men which was against the law. Publican Hosie illegally sold liquor to some working tribesmen. Several were shearers in their own tribal country opposite the Murrumbidgee junction, for James Hamilton of Narrung Station. Several other Wakool men were also shearers at another station on their own tribal land. The local press declared the shearers were maddened by brandy supplied to them at Hosie's Junction Hotel in Echuca.

They fought each other with tomahawks, sticks, spears and waddies. Three of the men were injured and were identified by their white names of Murray, Simon and Robert. Two weeks later Hosie was fined for supplying liquor to Aborigines.

Twenty years earlier their fathers were fighting the increasing number of white stockmen and squatters, using their spears and waddies effectively enough to drive some from their selected runs.

Chapter Seven

Corroboree at Moama 1864–1865

Along the Murray River the tribes were divided into two classes, the Makquarra (hawk) and the Kilparra (crow), with minor divisions of both, and marriages were arranged between the two classes. The mother's children followed her totem. These totems ceased at the Gippsland boundary of Kurnai country.[1]

The order of the hawk and crow was known to all the tribes of the Murray, but there were various totems within the clans. They served to prevent close marriages and even in death, the totems were important as the body was placed in the correct direction according to the area held by the group.[2]

John Atkinson, a descendant of the Yotti Yotta, spoke of the totem and the legends given to him and to other boys in the country of his birth:

'The tribal people had one marvellous thing that we have lost. That is the totem. They had the spiritual totem and the ordinary type totem and they seemed to fill in a wonderful part of their lives. Something that helped them work out their kinships. We have lost that. It seems such a pity and it is very sad. I have actually come up with two creatures I believe had something to do with the totem of our people.

'Along the Murray and Goulburn Rivers there are short-necked and long-necked turtles. They are still about and very plentiful too. I can remember when I was a small boy I wondered why I was allowed to eat the short-necked turtle, which was the 'stink turtle.' I'm sure most of the little kids of my age would have been mystified about that too. I realize now as I've grown older, the 'stink turtle' was like a skunk. He had organs in him that let off the stink when he was in danger. But of course as a little boy it always puzzled me that we ate it and not the long-necked turtle.

'I found out another interesting point about the short-necked turtle. He was obviously like a man. If he was in the water when a thunderstorm came and lightning struck the water, he would be killed because he had a negative and a positive in him. They were the glands that let off the stink. The old people called those glands thunder and lightning and when they cooked the turtle they took them out.

'I've heard my father speak of many occasions when he had been with the old men and they were diving for turtles. If they happened to be in a spot where all of a sudden the long-necked turtle appeared, they would get out of the water and walk away from that place. It must surely have been one of the totems belonging to them.

'Another creature I am sure was one of the totems was the frog-mouth owl. I think he's called the tawny frog-mouth owl. Looking back now, I can see he was one of the creatures that some of our old people thought was no longer any good trying telling us the meaning it held for the tribal group because, by then, they thought it didn't mean much to us. One thing they did tell us that if we pelted stones at the frog-mouth, or killed it, we would have very bad luck. So we never threw stones at them and we never did them any harm at all.'[3]

The breaking down of the full tribal culture relentlessly pursued its course with the disappearance of hunting grounds, increased sickness, deaths, and further gold discoveries. Miners used the Aboriginal people in every way possible, and if they were paid it was usually with cheap liquor. The common practice throughout Victoria in the squatting/gold era, and first selections years, was for an employer to present an Aboriginal worker with a bottle of home made grog, cheap wine, or a note to the local publican enabling the purchase of drink at the emloyers' expense. There was far more condemnation of any Aborigines seen drunk or drinking than for the white settlers in the same condition.

The brewery at Moama kept the liquor supplies flowing and Mr Greeman's accident on the premises, when the cork of a soda water bottle flew out with great violence and seriously damaged his eye, did not hinder business. The Echuca publicans reduced the price of nobblers from one shilling to six pence, to the great delight of those with a yen for a nobbler.

Echuca was not only the 'meeting place of the waters,' it was, and always had been, the meeting place for Aborigines. One of the Jaara tribesmen visited the town and decided to stay. He was twenty-three years old and known by everyone as Paddy Murphy. He was popular with the townspeople, a friend to all, and a familiar figure for two years. He died of consumption and the Riverine Herald lamented his passing, saying the sight of Paddy's good humoured face would be missed about the township.

Not long after Paddy's death in 1864 a visitor to Echuca commented on the sight of several tribesmen the worse for drink and with them a part-Aboriginal child. He questioned the possibility of something being done for Aboriginal children. A resident named Beth replied that the same comments were made in 1854, 'and still nothing has been done for the people whose country we inhabit and possess. Since our occupation of the water frontage has driven their means and subsistence further from their reach, regular assistance should be given to the very few of their old people who remain.'[4]

Beth's opinion was that Britain should do her duty towards the Aborigines because the Empire had gained so much from Australia. Referring to the children of mixed blood her suggestion was that their white fathers should be found and made to maintain their child or children.

The government had appointed a Protection Board four years earlier and now a number of men throughout the State were Honorary Correspondents. Their duty was to inform the Board on the health, numbers, and hereabouts of the Aborigines in their district. In the returns, the names of the Aborigines were listed who were given sugar and flour and sometimes a blanket. For the year of 1864, Police Magistrate C. Strutt had stores to distribute in Echuca which included thirty-six flannel shirts for women, thirty-six serge shirts for men, twenty-four blankets, and a bottle of castor oil.[5]

Possum and kangaroo skin cloaks were replaced with water-holding government blankets. Strutt informed the Board great numbers of native people died from illnesses arising from the cold winter months.[6] A considerable number had perished through violence due to the increase of conflict between tribal groups because their boundaries were swallowed up, disappearing forever into sheep and cattle station land.

The railway from Melbourne to Echuca was completed and the population grew on both sides of the river. So did disease amongst the tribes where the elders in most of the groups were attempting to hold on to their old life. They gave encouragement and example to the younger generation, instructing them about the sacred and entertaining corroborees, the exchange system of tools and food, the custom of initiation and the meetings of friendship.

The Jeithi walked across the plains from Deniliquin to join up at Moama with the families from the Yotti Yotta groups. They came from Shepparton, Mathoura and Kyabram. They came from the rivers and creeks, the swamps and lagoons, to the meeting place on the bank of the Murray at Moama, a spot where the tribes had met for unknown years. King Hopood's punt was no reason to change the site. Not yet. It was here that the last of the big corroborees took place.

The news spread that 150 tribal people had gathered and it was such a spectacular event that the Echuca townspeople crossed the river to watch the dancing and singing. Most of the white people there had never seen a corroboree and here would be no future opportunity.

The twenty-seven-year-old co-owner of an Echuca store would no doubt have taken his place in the throng of curious settlers. He was Daniel Matthews, and he had developed a keen interest in the Aborigines and knew many of their tribal and white names. He knew there would have been more tribal people for a corroboree before white occupation. Prior to moving to Echuca Matthews had contact with the Aborigines of Bendigo, Terrick Terrick Mount Hope, Gunnawrra, the Loddon River and the scattered tribal groups of the lower New South Wales country.

Owing to incursions and reprisals the native population had gradually become decimated.[7]

As the condition of the Yotti Yotta people grew worse with each day their cause was the subject of correspondence between Daniel Mathews and the Board of Protection of Aborigines.[8] He repeatedly brought attention to his idea of having a station on the Murray for them where they could live in peace but this was disregarded and Mathew sadly admitted, 'Alas it is beyond our power to awaken sympathy where it does not exist … It has often been remarked that Victoria's hope is in her youth. If so, what hope have we for the unfortunate children of these neglected blacks?[9]

Sympathy or not, the Aborigines had their uses for the Government of Australia. The Queensland Government recruited tribesmen from the Jeithi tribe for their Native Police Force. On one occasion Mathews saw a number of them en route to a punitive lifestyle against their own countrymen. The article covering the enlistment was published in the Sydney Morning Herald and reprinted in the Riverine Herald 27 September 1865.

There were twenty-two tribesmen, mainly from the Edward and Murrumbidgee Rivers and they had two comely dames with them. The men were all around the six feet mark with a manly and intelligent countenance and like many of their race, bear beneath their sable hue, singular resemblances to the peculiarities of different races. One is like a Spaniard, another Portuguese and another bearing much resemblance to a British Officer well-known in Sydney. They are in form and gait as fine fellows as would be picked up by a recruiting sergeant in an English county.

They were taken to Sydney by a recruiting officer and an elderly Queensland tribesman who had been in the Native Police force for fifteen years. The writer of the article was not altogether happy that the Jeithi men had entered the Queen's service and to be trained to pursue and fire with precision on their fellow countrymen, a work which may be necessary but it is not morally elevating. He remarked that such strapping fellows of muscular frames should have been taught road-making, clearing and fencing, rather than the career facing them. The Jeithi tribesmen and the two tribeswomen were taken from Sydney to Brisbane on the Cawarra.

Twenty-six years later a group of people on a trip to the Murrumbidgee district also had reason to comment on the size of the tribesmen who had inhabited that part of the country. The Riverine Herald published an account on 4 December 1891:

On one of the numerous creeks north-east of Balranald they found a skeleton, that of a tribesman who had been eight feet tall. They found, too a burial ground, and must surely have disturbed it somewhat as they said that all the men were buried in sitting positions and facing in an easterly direction. One of the party picked up a skull with seven distinct wounds. The men took the skeleton of the tribesman back with them to Tyson's Tupra Station near the Lachlan River.

Chapter Eight

Prosperity and Poverty 1865–1867

In the summer of 1865 bushfires roared along both sides of the Murray destroying many trees which bore the history of the tribes in the scars left by the removal of bark for canoes, shelters and dishes. Red gums that beat the fires fell to the axe and were sent by rail to help build Melbourne. Sheep stations had scab problems, and fires destroyed pastures.

Unlike the Aborigines who had maintained their food supply by moving from place to place in the tribal days, the settlers saw no need to preserve the animals and birds for breeding. The Echuca market was full every week with the wild ducks, geese and swans brought in from the backwaters to see to the townspeople, the swaggies and visitors. The trade in the birds increased to such a degree that the press became concerned, '… their numbers are getting thinned … is there no way to stop the wholesale slaughter?'[1]

The Echuca Port created a moving population and shady deals along the river brought dishonest, single, moneyless and homeless men to the towns on the river. They camped where it was the cheapest. One such man was J. Middleton who was charged with having no visible means of support. 'He lived chiefly on orange peel and had a country residence among the gum trees in the swamp where he chummed in with the blacks.'[2]

Apart from Melbourne, the port was the busiest in Victoria with thirty-five large steamers and about seventy barges using the facilities. During the wool season vessels arrived from South Australia and passengers and consignments of goods found their way to Queensland.[3]

The Victorian and New South Wales settlers had screamed for land. 'O, Rulers wise, 'tis justice cries that all may share the soil. Unlock the lands. There's willing hands that want but room to toil.'[4]

The result of the call for land was the Duffy Act.[5] Selectors moved in on properties held down for so long by the squatters. All manner of swindles, trickery, blackmail and bribery were unashamedly used by both selector and squatter. The latter bought the selectors' properties and as well gained ownership of thousands of acres by 'dummying.'[6] A squatter chose a man to select land for him with his financial assistance. The 'dummy' then promptly transferred the land to the squatter.

This caused hatred between the squatters and settlers who were sincere in their desire to select land. Sir John O'Shanassy, Victorian Premier, (1857; 1858–1859; 1861–1863) used two Aboriginal children as dummies in buying land at Moama, and hundreds of other wealthy men, including Hugh Glass, used similar tactics to hold their property and increase their acreage.[7]

Between 1861 and 1880 in the Murray electorate to the south of Deniliquin, of the twenty-one hundred persons who took up selections, five hundred and ninety remained in occupation.[8] Daniel and William Matthews selected 800 acres of frontage on John O'Shanassy's Moira lease, he being Sir John's son.[9]

Moira was called Moitheriban by the Yotti Yotta group and the property reached as far as the Murray west of Moama. The town had previously been part of the run. The Matthews' section was on the edge of an extensive forest reserve.[10] They did not change the name of the area as the Aborigines told them it was 'maloga' a place of sand hills. The Matthews' selection became known in southern New South Wales and Victoria as Maloga. It was one river frontage where the Aboriginal families could camp without being moved away.

The Aboriginal men were employed by overseers and owners of the stations as shearers, shepherds, wool pickers and washers, but it was pointed out in the press that this work, exposed them to the association of the lowest characters who infest the sheep and castle stations, men who were licentious and debauched.[11]

To accommodate the increased population during these seasons, in more ways than one, there was no shortage of grog-shops, brothels, pubs, and better class hotels. The Murray River Hotel in High Street, Echuca, next door to the office of *Riverine Herald* offered,

> Best meals in town, including soup and pudding for one shilling. A patent machine on the counter for heating grog and beer. No extra charge for hot drinks. A bright fire blazing in the bar.
>
> The proprietor of the Echuca Hotel also in High Street, opposite Shackell's bonded stores had this to say he,
>
> Begs to inform his friends and the public that he has opened the above hotel and hopes, by strict attention, to merit a share of their support. A choice selection of old wines and spirits. Stabling for twenty horses.
>
> And for those who were journeying to, or past, Mathoura, Henry Burton advised that his Red Bank Hotel
>
> Half way between Echuca and Deniliquin had first class accommodation for families and gentlemen. Beautiful garden and vineyard. Fishing and shooting. Good stabling and attentive grooms. Cobb and Co's coaches daily.

Denilakoon was the name of a Jeithi tribesman who was famous for his wrestling prowess. In 1842 a London stockbroker named Benjamin Boyd arrived in Australia. He became one of the largest landholders amongst the squatters including one area he called Deneliquin.

Men and women from all parts of the world quenched their thirst at the town and back-block hotels. The labourers knocked down their pay packets and most were very obliging in assisting their Aboriginal workmates to knock their pay down as well. Daniel Matthews said there was an absolute necessity for immediate action to suppress the strong drink sold to the tribesmen during their prolonged visits to the towns. Unlimited supplies of gin and beer were made available to them while they paid cash.

Matthews expressed his views vocally and in the press, regarding the Aborigines' right to have land of their own where they could live, receive farm training and schooling for the children as well as adults. Eventually in 1866 he drew a response from the Victorian Government. A grant would be made of some acres on the river near Echuca, the site to be selected by Board members where buildings, including a schoolhouse, would be built.

That year slipped away without any firm agreement and the New Year of 1867 was celebrated by the white owners of Echuca and its surrounds. Festivities took place on The Strip and the newspaper announced happily that the revelers were too drunk to do much harm. They were the happy drunks.[12]

Aboriginal boys from ten to young men of twenty were rapidly dying out in the neighbourhood of his station Mr. A. McKenzie of Wyuna said. He was at Reedy Creek, fourteen miles from Echuca on the lower Goulburn River. These young men could not withstand the ravages of spirits which they obtained through the white men in the towns. He said they earned money in bush jobs, '… then drink spirits, eat very little, and lie down and die … God knows that some of us, I think I may say that the great majority of the squatters, are sincerely anxious that these poor people, the first inheritors of the land, should be saved from perishing.'[13]

Daniel Matthews realized early in his occupation of Maloga that it was the meeting and camping place for the Yotti Yotta and had been for generations and although the Matthews' farming interests were known to the Aborigines they continued to hold onto their traditional customs while they were at Maloga. They gathered there in hundreds and Matthews became their friend. In the many cases of illness and the need for clothing when they moved amongst the white community, they recognized in him a man who sympathized with, and helped, the families.

When the tribesmen told him they would like to sit down at a permanent camp and engage in farm labour Matthews engaged a solicitor at his own expense and collect nearly fifty local residents' signatures and presented the petition to the Government, asking for the land already referred to for the Aborigines. He had a long wait for his reply.

Matthews offered rations to Sally, one of the young Aboriginal women, if she would wash and iron his laundry. He proudly showed her work to friends. Some weeks after when Sally was still performing her duties as Matthews laundress, a wife of one of his friends gave him a fashionable crinoline dress for one of the tribeswomen. He thought Sally had earned a better reward than the usual ration so he presented her with the dress. She wore it but the crinoline was definitely a cage for birds and she put it aside. Matthew asked his friend to dress Sally in the approved manner, cage included, and Sally was so happy with her appearance she walked to Echuca and had her photo taken at the photographers.

Thirty years later, Daniel Matthews still had Sally's photograph and declared it was 'proof that vanity is not confined to the white race.'[14]

While Sally was so delighted with her crinoline dress there were white men and women exchanging food with her people for their possum and kangaroo rugs and cloaks to add to their collections of native implements, either bought or acquired. A convict living in Echuca and working his time out as a ticket-of-leave holder was charged with stealing a possum rug from one of the settlers, having been caught escaping with it across the river into New South Wales. The settler told the magistrate she valued the rug at twenty-five shillings, and the thief was sent off to gaol for three months.

The floods in 1867 were declared to be the worst ever experienced by the white residents along the river as the water flowed through Echuca swamping shops, hotels, houses and land. The original residents informed them the Murray and the Campaspe had met a long time ago where the railway terminus stood.

The next month Police Magistrate Strutt reported that the general condition of the Aborigines in his district continued without any material alteration. Matthews was noticeably desperate for the improvement of their situation and, in particular, the circumstances of one of the children touched him to the point that he brought her into his own home at Malogy.

He had Sally clothe her in suitable dresses and he made time to give her school lessons. The child was Jemima Burns. He afterwards took Jemima to the Coranderrk Aboriginal Station in Healesville. In the years prior to 1867 several other young men and women had been taken from Echuca and placed in the Government Station named Coranderrk.

The ever increasing number of paddle steamers on the Murray made life more difficult for the Yotti Yotta groups who fished the river for cod, yellow belly, redfin and cray.

An American named Gus Peirce was a Captain on the river steamers. During his first two years he said there were numerous 'blackfellars camps' along the river where he bartered with them, replenishing his larder with geese and ducks' eggs in exchange for tobacco and flour. At the Moira Lake he watched the men paddling about in their bark canoes spearing fish. Some of the catch they cooked over the small fires they kept alight with dry grass and leaves in the bottom of the craft.

Peirce commented on the increase of white men fishing and timber cutting about the area. They fished from dugouts they made by scooping out the interior of tree trunks. Useable, though very heavy boats, he decided.

Chapter Nine

A Changing, Shrinking World 1868–1879

The squatters and settlers fenced their extensive properties and the Aboriginal people found their tribal countries divided by chock-and-log, post and rail. Long established stock routes were cut off and this forced detours with stock into tribal lands not yet completely alienated from the original owners. The tribes were losing ground and waterways.

Some of the Moitheraban watched the captains of the river steamers, Wahgunyah and Cumberoona, ease their vessels carefully along The Narrows, between the Moira and Barmah Lakes where the river poured through a channel which in places was only thirty yards wide.[1]

The tribesmen saw the Wahgunyah returning to Echuca from Corowa when the Cumberoona forced her way past the smaller vessel. She crashed the paddle boxed and as she cleared, the trailing barge on the Cumberoona hit the Wahgunyah's stern. The bargeman was thrown under the paddle steamers. His body was never recovered.[2]

Captain Gus Peirce described the narrow channel as very deep, and winding for some twelve miles between two thickly timbered ridges which separated it on both sides from the large lakes which were sometimes connected by swamps. The Aborigines knew this was where the Murray Cod spawned. During the high water in the wet seasons the lakes rose, joined with the river and formed one large sheet of water, Lake Moira. Peirce said during the high water the channel was distinctly marked out by the tops of the trees.[3]

The Moitheriban families who lived in these parts of their territory about the lakes were often visited by Matthews, usually with a bag of sweets in his pocket for the children. He was just as concerned for the Towrooban people at Towro which was the name of a portion of a sandhill between the Madowla Lagoon and the Murray. They specialised in possum hunting, and were expert in making fishing weirs but respected the ownership of channels and sections of the area which belonged to theWongatpan. Both these groups pierced the septum of the nose and inserted bones. They scarred their bodies, had restrictions on certain foods, and, included in their culture, was the knocking out of the young boys' front teeth.

The Kailtheban people of the Kaiela (Goulbourn River) knew Matthews as he visited their camps along the river. Their country included Shepparton and Kyabram. They were excellent swimmers and when the river was clear they dived after the fish with their short barbed spears. Sometime they threw branches of young gum trees into small lagoons and when the eucalyptus oil reduced the fish to insensibility they waded into the water and gathered them very easily.

The Murray River was too busy now for the spun grass fishing nets but the Moira Lakes Aborigines still made them to use in quieter waters. They did this by taking the fibrous root of the balyan, (bulrush) peeled off the outer rind and left the root for some time in the ashes of the fire. Then they twisted and loosened it by hand, and finished by chewing the root until a small ball of fibre remained. This was drawn out and rubbed on the thigh with the palm of the hand, and after some twisting and pulling the string was formed ready to make the nets.

Many times Matthew saw the finished product suspended across the water and tied with grass rope to the high limbs of the red gums. Sometimes it was a family affair to net the flocks of ducks or swans. On those occasions, as soon as the game was spotted, one of the men whistled, imitating the notes of a hawk and the whole terrified flock would swoop to avoid the killer bird, and become entangled in the net.[4]

Great cheers of delight and laughter always filled the air after a successful catch but the tribal laws had to be obeyed. Some of the fish which were snared in a new net could not be eaten by the girls as they would break out with red sunning sores.[5]

At time when the adults were netting, the children did their own hunting by skillfully spearing frogs, iguanas, snakes and water rats.

However, all was not serene. Timber cutters' camps and mills mushroomed in the forests as the huge red gums crashed. Fishermen's shacks dotted the banks of the rivers and creeks, and although some of the tribal men worked for the professional fishermen expecting wages, they often received alcohol instead, as in Victoria.

Daniel Matthews was determined to right some of the wrongs and when, in 1869, there was no sign of the reserved land for the Aborigines he visited England to get financial assistance from his older brother to fund a Mission. He failed.[6]

The following year he and his brother, William, gave up twenty acres of Maloga Station to establish a school for the Aboriginal children. Matthews walked and rode around the camps to tell the tribespeople his intentions. Some of the children were consumptive, others had contracted hydatids from the creeks and streams which were fouled by stock and dogs. Even so, Matthews estimated there could be twenty children who would attend the school but he needed a building apart from the school, a house for them to live in at Maloga.

In 1872 he was still trying to raise finance when he married twenty-three year old Janet Johnston. He was thirty-five.[7]

Livestock from the Riverina district crossed the Murray for the Victorian market, and the activities on the sheep stations for hundreds of miles around intensified as their wool clips multiplied. The stations took on the appearance of small, but busy, townships. Most of them had a 'Blacks' Camp' and the owners drew on the men for labour. There were also, 'the women's camps,' where in too any instances, young tribal girls were kept for the sexual pleasures of the employees as well as for the owners and their sons.

It was not until 1873 that Matthew had a schoolhouse to double-up for sleeping quarters, ready for us. It was into the next year before there was official recognition of Daniel Matthews' Maloga Mission, 'for the improvement of the condition of the Aborigines.' It was described in later years as the first systematic and successful effort made on behalf of the Aborigines of New South Wales.[8]

Daniel and Janet Matthews began their work with four children and an adult couple.[9] The number on the Mission built rapidly, added to by thirteen Queensland tribal people who had been left stranded in Sydney.[10]

Mathews gathered young girls and boys from the camps and his wife taught them in the school. Although at first their parents objected. The demands for the return of the children were overcome through his kindness to them. Some of the families followed their children to Maloga and camped on their traditional ground to be near them.[11]

Trouble loomed when conflict between Matthews and station owners surfaced over the loss of cheap labour as the people moved to Maloga. Two squatters in particular on both sides of the Murray with whom Matthews had trouble with were John O'Shanassy of Moria Station and Robert Kinnear from Madowla Park. This had been part of the Lower Moira run where Edward Curr pastured his stock in the 1840s between the Murray and the Goulburn Rivers and Barmah Forest. Matthews had no time for the two men and spoke strongly about their use of free labour.

When he discovered one of the very young girls at Maloga was pregnant to a squatter all fury broke loose. The man admitted giving the child drink and sleeping with her all night in the bush near Barmah. The Board for the Protection of Aborigines in Melbourne was notified but the secretary advised Matthews nothing could be done because the girl came across the river from New South Wales.[12]

The squatter was asked by the local police sergeant, on behalf of the Board, what he was prepared to pay for the girl's maintenance and that of the child.[13]

This young girl and her baby were the first of the Aborigines to be given a home at Maloga Mission.

Snagging steamers methodically moved up and down the Murray and Goulburn clearing them for river transport. Some members of the Kailtheban of the Goulburn were living in their camps at Maloga when part of their river was taken over by the paddle steamboat Emily Jane in 1875.The Goulburn Advertiser told readers on 11 November that she was the first to undertake a trip on the Goulburn from Echuca to Shepparton. The wheat trade between Shepparton and Echuca was under full steam.

The wheat trade continued until 1888, and ironically, the last steamer to make the journey was the Waradgery, named after the Wiradjuri Tribe, neighbours of the Jeithi. The ownership of their country covered Albury, Wagga Wagga, Narrandera and Griffith and further afield, but their people were in distress. They, too, were making their last trip.

As the Matthews' station was owned between the brothers Daniel found money was sometimes not too plentiful in his household especially when their own children were born. He was careful not to have the Aboriginal men work on his property as he had no money to pay them, so some worked outside Maloga, branding and shearing for other station owners.

He continued to ask government to provide land so that the people could be self supporting. In the meantime the Aboriginal families and his own had happy times camping in the Barmah Forest which, he said, served to relieve the confinement of the mission.[14]

They hunted the kangaroos, emus, possums, and caught the black swans and the ducks. When a red kangaroo was cooked the young girls and boys were not allowed to eat the meat. They could enjoy the crayfish and the luscious grubs they chopped out of the trees with their tomahawks.

They sat around the campfires and roasted the food, often just thrown on top of the charcoal embers or buried in hot ashes to cook. Sometimes the game was coated with clay and roasted in hole in the sand. Matthews knew these idyllic days would become fewer as sickness and death moved onto Maloga.

The white names of some of the Aboriginal people who were residents during the early years of the Maloga Mission were:

Atkinson. Anderson. Atwood. Alton. Barber. Boyd. Barnes. Brangy. Billy. Company. Cooper. Clements. Charles. Clark. Cameron. Daylight. Hall. Howard. Jackson. Keefe. Morgan. Murray. McCrae. Middleton. Oney. Russell. Stuckey. Swift. Simpson. Smythe. Toodle. Kennedy. Reeve. Vincent. Walker.

More non-Aboriginal names appeared on official records as white settlement was becoming firmly established with such people as Mr Burrrerley. He was the landlord of the Shamrock Hotel in Deniliquin. He was returning home on the Hay road when he was stuck up by two robbers. They tied him to a tree, took his money, and left him there all night.

Then there were the murmurings from the good but unhappy congregation of St Paul's Church. True, the verger was a very amiable looking fellow but he allowed dogs in the church during Divine Service! It was not so bad if they were content to lie quietly but they barked and growled, bit at their fleas, and worse, they followed the collector menacingly. The churchgoers announced it was high time it all stopped.

Chapter Ten

Maloga, the Mission 1880–1887

They were not eased out from tribal lands with compassion. They were usurped, often with brutality.

> I do not call the killing of whites by the blacks murder … in many instances they had great provocation.[1]

Victorian graziers were well ensconced in the areas bounded by the rivers Goulburn, Campaspe and Murray. In southern New South Wales the sheep men were settled in the lush river district and spread across the fertile lands of grass where the native trees were open forest. However, they worked on the principle that each tree that towered above meant less wool. Every tree was ring-barked and properties cleared. More wool was loaded on wagons pulled by draught horses or bullocks and trundled across the plains to the Murray steamboats going to Echuca. The last stage was reached when the wool was dispatched by rail to Melbourne.

With all the hectic maneuvering on the river Echuca developed into the largest inland port in Australia. Several extensions to the wharf were built until, in the 1880s, it was over half a mile long. The wharf was as big as the thirst of the old diggers, the gamblers, the assortment of unsavoury characters, and the riverboat crew who landed them. Townspeople were familiar with the sound of the slosh and whack of the steamer paddles, the hoot-blowing, and the smell of spiralling smoke mixed with the odour of wool on the waiting barges.

They did not take so kindly to the brawls and brawn on display along the waterfront, or the hotels nearby that provided food and beds for the night and took care of their patrons' thirsts. Flocker Liz and a few other ladies of the night and day looked after everything else. It was not long before Echuca was famous for eighty odd pubs.

In contrast, Matthews was in daily contact with the few tribes people gathered on the meager landholding of Maloga. He saw the men making hunting weapons and tools, binding stone to wood with heated gum from the river trees, and he noticed the older men at times used strong threads from spiders' webs for a much neater job. He learned about the tribal medical remedies and healing powers as old as the race itself. For this, the women collected the necessary herbage and he and his wife marvelled at the cures resulting from the special preparations using eucalyptus leaves, roots, plants, flowers and shrubs.

Lubra's Camp at Maloga. (Courtesy Jean Cross.)

The Aborigines had strict marriage laws prior to white occupation and if the rules were broken the offender was severely punished, but after forty-six years of constant European influence Matthews said their racial laws were impaired. One of the first acts of reform he adopted at Maloga was to induce them to marry according to British laws. They objected, saying they had been married enough. Several prospective brides and grooms belonging to one of the Yotti Yotta groups decided to marry each other in their own tribal way, refusing Matthews method. He promptly locked the storeroom door and refused food to the couples unless they agreed to a European marriage. 'After a few days of conference and empty stomachs, a deputation waited upon me with the information that they were willing to get married.'[2]

Janet and Daniel knew Annie, a part-Aboriginal girl who lived with her family on the Murray until she was ten years old. At that early age she was taken into the home of white settlers to work for them. When she was in her mid teens Annie became pregnant to an Echuca paddle steamer crewman. Her employer wanted her out of the way and sent her to the Lake Condah Aboriginal Reserve in the Western District of Victoria.

After the birth of her son the father wanted her to return to the Murray and live with him in Echuca. She was given permission to return to Echuca on condition that she married the man. Three years later Annie was still at Lake Condah but wanted to leave and work outside to earn her own living.

Annie's case was similar to dozens along the Murray, Campaspe, Darling, Edward and Murrumbidgee Rivers. Matthews brought their plight to the notice of the settlers and Governments in Victoria and New South Wales through his correspondence, private and published. A letter written by E. W. Palmer, the Secretary of the Aborigines Protection Association in New South Wales was given space in the Deniliquin press:

> These poor girls seldom reach the age of fifteen before they are ruined in the most ruthless manner and, sad to relate, the wrong is done, not by the swagmen and lower classes of bushmen only, but by men occupying respectable positions in society – men who claim the title of 'gentlemen' but who are so devoid of every gentle feeling that they can stand aloof while their own offspring are debased to the lowest depths. Is it not proof of the maternal love and instinct of the poor lubras of the Murray and Murrumbidgee that in all their degradation and semi-starvation they would devote their energies to rear their babies born under such circumstances. Let the facts plead their own cause. Will not the churches rouse themselves to end this sad story.[3]

Palmer believed too many people had made up their minds the Aborigines were dying out and shut their eyes to the fact that it was the white race,

> … killing the Aborigines by encouraging them in the most odious vices … If the clergy had done their proper work, the pulpits would have resounded from Sunday to Sunday with pleas for the Aboriginal …[4]

The Sydney News joined in the controversy writing that the one disgrace of Australian settlement was the manner in which the Aborigines had been treated, '… and it is feared that we are still very blameworthy in neglecting the remnant that is left of the tribes that once roamed over New South Wales.'

It was mainly through Matthews influence on members of parliament that the New South Wales Aborigines Protection Association was formed in 1880. Because of his constant barrage of published articles, letters and addresses to anyone who would listen to him, the predicament of the Aborigines remained as a festering sore, waiting to be healed.

The Aborigines came from Victoria and New South Wales to the Maloga Mission. Some camped on the sand hills as in the old days, and left again, but their hunting days were over when they could roam without the barriers of fences, fish the rivers without the paddle steamers churning the water and scattering their bark canoes and fish.

> Oh! River, glorious river! Changed am I, but so art thou; I see thy waters dashed aside by many a venturous prow; and hideous shrieks of whistling steam in every reach and rest, where long ago the bark canoe seemed dreaming on thy breast.[5]

The tribal people were dying Matthews stated, and on the death of one of their number they do not mention his or her name again but they did speak with fear and respect about the Great Spirit they called Baimai. The old people made sure they were safely camped before dark as the evil spirits wandered about at night. 'All the superstitions and prejudices had passed out of the lives of the young native, but the older ones retain them.'[6]

The urgency to know more about the Australian Aborigines spread outside the continent and in 1881 an eminent Paris scientist visited Maloga Mission and examined the people. He measured them and noted the colour of their skin and the texture of their hair and concluded, in an announcement, he allied them to the Aborigines of Central India.

The Mission financial situation was always in a bad state. Private contributions and occasional Government aid was not enough so at times of difficulty Matthews took to the road collecting clothes, toys, books and money. His friend, Reverend John Gribble, had commenced the Warangesda Mission in Wiradjuri country on the Murrumbidgee. The site was west of Narrandera and three miles from Darlington Point. He, too, travelled the country looking for support. The white communities said these men were wasting time and money educating the Aborigines. It would not be long before they were all dead.[7]

Warangesda Mission Site. (Courtesy G. Barber.) "The Avenue". Row of pepper trees planted by Mrs Edward's uncle and others about 1920. The roadway was formerly the main entrance to the mission from the Narrandera-Hey road.

There were other reasons for non-support of the Warangesda Mission. Prior to Gribble's arrival in their midst, the Wiradjuri women were helpless in warding off the sexual attacks of white men who came to their camps in the bush. Once the mission was established the situation changed. One day a stationhand, in rage and frustration, rode into the Mission Square swinging a stirrup iron demanding the removal of the Mission and threatening death to any person who came near him.

Undeterred, Gribble brought and encouraged the Aborigines to the Mission. Others, as at Maloga, went there voluntarily or for tribal reasons, erected their mia-mias and set up their camps on the Murrumbidgee. Once, when Gribble was away from the Mission he discovered on his return a gentleman had brought a case of gin to the women's camp. 'At another time the keeper of a low bush hotel supplied the camp with drink, called in the white men around and, as an eye witness informed me, the scene was a little hill. The following morning I visited the camp and there I witnessed a most revolting sight. Poor old women and quite young girls helplessly drunk,' A young mother told Gribble they were forced to drink the spirits.[8]

Warangesda Mission. Dormitory, side view.

As Daniel Matthews was a public school teacher his salary per annum was 168 pounds. He spent his wages for the benefit of the Mission where his school and pupils progressed satisfactorily. There were white settlers' children on most of the Aboriginal Reserves who also received their education. Victoria had hundreds of non-Aboriginal children who were left without any schooling.

An average of eighty people made their home at Maloga Mission where everyone gathered for morning prayers. Mathews expected his rules to be obeyed, one of which was no alcohol on the mission. Maloga had become a tiny village with the school house which was also used at meal times, six huts for married couples, a storeroom, separate dormitories for the young girls and boys, and the single women and men.

When the Matthews had visitors they spent some of their time working on the Mission. People wishing to see the Mission were welcomed, some gave donations, others their labour. Three visiting ladies remained on the mission. They were Mrs Edwards as Matron to help Janet when the people were ill and Miss Peram of Melbourne and Miss Rainey from Dublin as assistant teachers.[9]

In 1881 Matthews accepted an offer made to him by a twenty-five year old Indian man to teach in the mission school. He was from Mauritious and became known as Thomas Shadrach James. They met when Matthews had taken forty-one Aborigines from Maloga to a renewal camp at Brighton Beach, not far out from Melbourne.[10]

Thomas Shadrach James had been studying to be a medical practitioner but was forced to terminate his studies when he contracted typhoid. He became a qualified school teacher.[11] As Matthews assistant, he began forty years of valued service to the Aboriginal community as a teacher in the mission school, a recognized State (Public) School. During that same year a Protector of Aborigines was appointed in New South Wales with funds to the extent of a few hundred pounds for mission schools.[12]

In the following year Edmond Fosbery, Inspector-General of Police, and Philip Gidley King, Member of the Legislative Council, were sent as Commissioners to inquire into Maloga and Warangesda. They saw the men had to work away from the Missions for farmers and graziers, but hunt kangaroos in order to provide for their families. They agreed more aid should be made available but disapproved of Matthews system of control over the villagers, especially when he expelled any who disobeyed rules.

The government men believed a suspension of privileges should serve the purpose.

By now the Matthews brothers' land was long since liable to forfeiture by non-payment of interest and King and Fosbery recommended about 2,000 acres of forest reserve be appropriated, including the brothers' Maloga Station. They were not in favour of abandoning Maloga as the land was well suited for a station. By forming a Government Station, the Aborigines could be further trained, and the necessary additional buildings built by the Maloga people.[13]

It was stated in Parliament that a number of children at Maloga Mission were as white as any Honourable and should be taken from their mothers and trained in specially provided institutions. No one objected on the grounds of inhumanity. During the same debate one member said it was inhumane when Queensland tribesmen were kidnapped to be taken to America.[14]

The Aborigines who tried to live outside missions by hunting when there was only seasonal work with settlers, were unable to find a sufficient quantity of food and at times the families were famished for days.This drew them to the already struggling Maloga Mission. The reports eventually forced the Government of New South Wales to establish a Protection Board in 1883. Matthews reinforced his plea for land for the exclusive use of the Aborigines.

When he learned the new policy being formed by the Government was to merge the part-Aborigines into the white population he was angry and distrustful and was not slow to remind Government and public that, '… poison, the bullet, the rum bottle, disease, unknown before the advent of our race have each shared in the work of spoilation.' He resigned as school teacher on the Mission and the New South Wales Department of Public Instruction appointed Thomas Shadrach James in his place.[15]

Matthews was in trouble with the Board for the Protection of Aborigines in Melbourne. The members frowned on his methods of care for the people and they knew of his dislike for the new policy. The rules on the mission still applied but the younger generation wanted more freedom and objected to some of the rules. This suited a number of settlers who wanted cheap workers and they continuously talked against Matthews and the Mission. Word reached Sydney and the Government ordered that finance records be made available for scrutiny and Matthews refused to comply.[16]

At last, with the help of petitions signed by the residents of Maloga Mission and sent to the Government of New South Wales, 1800 acres for the use of the Aborigines was gazetted in 1883. It was river frontage property opposite the Victorian township of Barmah where the forests of great red gums rose to 200 feet.[17] White people disagreed; the land was too good for an Aboriginal Reserve. As the move was not made for another five years they had time to get used to the idea.

In the meantime Matthews was the official Superintendent of the Mission, and the Aborigines Protection Association provided some necessary funding for the administration. He had always encouraged sports as a recreation amongst the splendid runners and strong, agile wrestlers. Sporting events became a frequent entertainment, fostering friendships and respect between the Aboriginal and white population. The cricket match at Barmah on a hot day in February 1884 was no exception. With Matthews as batsman, the Maloga men played the Bohemians, and won.

Wedding bells rang out at the Mission the following year when Thomas Shadrach James married one of his pupils, Ada Cooper. He was accepted gladly by her people. These were good times at the Mission; new huts, a new school; musical evenings, food rations and full stomachs.[18]

There were episodes that took place that were not good. Jack Briggs and his wife and family lived on the Maloga Mission until they went to Coranderrk, the Victorian Government Aboriginal Station at Healesville. The tribal word, coranderrk, was the native name for the profusion of Christmas Bushes growing in the area. When Briggs and other men asked for farming land at the station in 1885 they were termed trouble makers and ordered to leave.

The Briggs children were held at Coranderrk and when the Briggs couple returned to Maloga, Mrs Briggs wrote to the secretary of the Board in Melbourne, Reverend F. Hagenauer, and asked for the return of their children.

She was told under the power of the Act her children had to stay at Coranderrk for the present. Hagenauer said, '… when you and Jack are settled down and can support them that will be time enough to take them …'[19]

For two more years Maloga Mission continued with very little funding. More systematic management of Maloga was advocated by the far away government.[20]

Janet and Daniel raised money by taking the Maloga Band on tour. In 1887 when the Melbourne Board received a letter from a woman resident asking for clothing, saying, ' … we are half naked …' a new world soon opened to the Aborigines.[21]

Chapter Eleven

Cumeroogunga, a Prelude 1888–1889

To the survivors of the Yotti Yotta groups the word, kumeroogunja, meant 'to be raised.' A fitting name for their new home on the Murray. They had been assured their status in life would, indeed, be raised. They were promised their own blocks of land to farm at Cumeroogunga.

Due to the long drawn out battles launched by Daniel Matthews with Government bodies on both sides of the river regarding the Maloga property, land for the Aborigines and funding, and other causes he embraced, his position as Superintendent of Maloga Mission was withdrawn. A man named George Bellenger was installed as manager for the new station. The New South Wales Aboriginal Protection Association had no further use for Matthews.

The people were transferred from Maloga Mission to the land fought for, and won, by Mathews and his Aboriginal friends. Some of them stayed with Mathews and his family at Maloga and refused to make the move.

Thomas Shadrach James was appointed school teacher for Cumeroogunga. Approximately 120 Aboriginal people commenced another period of history at kumeroogunja, four miles away from their beloved Maloga. They were joined by James, his wife and children. The Government Reserve was on the New South Wales side of the river, half a mile from Victorian Barmah.

Manager Bellenger knocked down most of the houses, the bark huts and other buildings at Maloga and had them taken to Cumeroogunga to rebuild. When the doctor from Echuca saw the reserve he referred to it as 'the camp.' The people were without enough housing and lived in all sorts of make-do shelters of canvas and bark. The sanitary facilities were practically non-existent and he left instructions for Bellenger to repair the situation.

During the summer permission was granted for some of the people to camp again at Brighton as they had done with Matthews when they first met Shadrach James. This time the holiday turned into a nightmare as excessive rains drenched their camps, clothing and themselves; Little Mary Stuckey died from burns she received in the beach campfire; others became sick after being soaked and this caused the death of eighteen months old Clara Anderson. The sick and worried adults began the return trip home but twenty year old Annie Cooper was too ill to continue and she died in the hospital at Sandhurst.

The months moved on. The slab huts were still unfinished and unhygienic holes in the ground served as toilets. There were no streets in the settlement and no drainage. The state of the children's health and the dreadful condition of 'the camp' caused the medical officer, Dr Eakins of Echuca, to order Shadrach to close the school.

Typhoid fever killed one year old Edith Stuckey and two weeks later John Atkinson, just two years old, also died from the disease. Typhoid with tuberculosis took two year old Robert Cooper. Others with typhoid were Leonard Kerr, Henry Foster, Bertha Murray, Eliza Murray and William Charles.[1]

Bellinger said the typhoid had been brought back to the settlement by the Aborigines who had visited Melbourne, but the doctor pointed out that his instructions regarding the sanitary arrangements had been disregarded. He was angry with the manager and told the Board, '… Thomas James, the teacher, shows great willingness to help me with sanitary reforms.'[2]

Most of the women and children were sick. Some of the illnesses they had were ulcers, pneumonia, dyspepsia, hydatis, diarrhea and consumption. There were no disinfectants and nursing care was unavailable. The only medicines at Cumeroogunga, which were of no use at all, were kept in a small medical chest. After the doctor's next visit he asked the Board if a nurse could be provided from the Bendigo Hospital. Two month later he had not heard from the Board Committee.[3]

The Aboriginal people told Dr Eakins about the poor quality of food given to them as rations for working on the reserve. He agreed with them and described the sugar as more like inferior cement. He told the Board that the milk doled out to the families was totally inadequate and asked that instructions be wired to the manager for additional milk, '… it is more than a farce to pretend to help the sick if no nourishment is made available.' He informed the Board that the camp was completely disorganized and there was a great deal of discontent and disapproval of the management.[4]

The residents had an intense dislike for Bellenger and had every good reason for their attitude. When one of the children died in the hospital at Echuca the parents asked him if they could use the station buggy to take the body to their burial place in the sand hills of Maloga. He refused.

Bellenger refused rations to a family when the father did not work on the station but cared for his children because the mother was ill with consumption. No work, no rations! He then poisoned their two dogs. For this he was summoned and the Bench gave a verdict against him.

He refused rations to a number of the more healthy Aborigines because they disobeyed his orders. Bellenger was in full command of the Government Reserve and was backed by members of the Aboriginal Protection Association in New South Wales. His word was law on Cumeroogunga.

A nurse had at last been sent to the settlement and Dr Eakins advised the immediate removal of the healthy families to a camp a mile away. Later on when he visited Cumeroogunga he found conditions were so bad he called in the local police to make Bellenger carry out his orders for cleaning up the settlement. '… He sent the rest of the healthy people back to Maloga to escape the infection.'[5]

Back to Maloga was an unpopular direction made by the doctor as the Association felt Matthews had always preached too much and had not made money out of mission resources. The Chairman of the Protection Board remarked that Bellenger, '… does not seem a fit person to have charge of the Mission station

…' The Association was asked what action would be taken in reference to the typhoid and other sickness at the reserve.[6] The doctor was replaced!

As Bellenger had taken all the buildings from Maloga, Matthews had trouble in finding shelter for the so far healthy residents from Cumeroogunga. Bellenger refused to send any tents to help ease the situation and would only supply them if the people all returned to 'his' station. So it was back to Cumeroogunga and Bellenger, much to Matthews' regret. He gave the people fruit and vegetables from Maloga, and sympathy. Manager Bellenger banned Daniel Matthews from visiting the Aborigines at Cumeroogunga.

The manager lived comfortably in the rebuilt hospital from Maloga, now a converted four roomed house.

Deaths and discontent were ongoing until, in frustration, nineteen residents signed a letter to the Board asking for the removal of the causes for their dissatisfaction which, they said, '…have for long been robbing us of our peace and impeding our progress as a community.' They knew under the rules of the Protection Association, no man was entitled to rations for his family unless he worked six hours a day. Many of the men were sick with consumption and could not work. It was up to Bellenger to decide which men would receive rations.

The letter told the Board they regretted they could not ever work in harmony with the manager as he treated them badly during the present troubled times of sickness. 'We receive neither pay, help or sympathy.'[7]

Sam Barber was two years old when he died of typhoid at Coranderrk. Caroline Morgan had taken her baby Maria, to Coranderrk. Maria was ill, and died. Both children were buried at Coranderrk, said to have died from the effects of colds.

During 1889 the men ringbarked the trees on 400 acres of the reserve. A village began to take shape with one store and a butcher's shop. The Maloga Mission School became the Cumeroogunga Church and the meeting house was the school where fifty-two children attended daily. There were eighteen cottages to house 134 residents.

Most of the men worked on the reserve waiting and hoping for their own promised blocks. When there was no work, so no rations, they earned money by shearing, rabbitting and hunting. Of the 1,890 acres, 400 were high sand-hills above the river level and suitable for agriculture. The rest was low-lying box country with the usual amount of gum swamp along the river. The whole area was fenced with 100 acres cleared and cultivated, growing wheat, barley and hay. The men enclosed a three acre orchard with a rabbit proof fence.

John (Sandy) Atkinson.

The Matthews kept the Maloga Mission operating and the Aborigines were always welcome which brought a comment from the Melbourne based General Inspector of Aborigines for Victoria, Reverend F. Hagenauer. 'Mr D. Matthews is determined to keep up Maloga in opposition to Cumeroogunga.' Even though the outlaw missionary held Sunday services, Bellenger forbade the Aboriginal people to attend, nor could Matthews conduct any services at Culmeroogunga.

In the first summer weeks of 1889 the townspeople of Echuca and Moama had complained about the white men who swam in the river and paraded in daring attire on the sand bank adjacent to the saw mills and the Echuca wharf. Their language was not acceptable either and it was suggested the Victorian Police should put a stop to such shocking behavior.

The days were far away when the first settlers objected to the state of undress of the tribal people who swam and speared fish in the same spot.

Chapter Twelve

Cumeroogunga Farmers 1890–1899

The 1890s collapse of banks and building societies combined with other factors brought Victoria to a split in the road to financial prosperity, and the depression which followed covered a decade. The graziers could not get their price for wool, the dairy farmers' produce was effected in the same way and, in turn, shearers' and labourers' wages were cut. Unemployment and strikes raged throughout the State.

Into this cooking pot of unrest walked the 'released' part-Aboriginal people of Victoria. It was announced triumphantly that the Merging Policy was complete! These people, under thirty-four years of age, were sent into the general community to assimilate. They were turned out of their homes on Mission and Government Reserves. Families were separated. They were told they were officially white people irrespective of the colour of their skin or their background as inmates on Aboriginal Reserves always under the authority of a manager, a non-Aboriginal man.

Without any worthwhile training work was usually impossible to find. Because of the lack of homes, work, money and food, many of these Aboriginal people from all over Victoria turned for help to Matthews at Maloga. Once again he brought down the anger of Hagenauer upon his head, being accused of encouraging and receiving the Aborigines on his property.

The men who were permitted, and or forced, to remain at Cumeroogunga urged the authorities to give them the legal rights to the land they cleared, worked and fenced, but they and their families were just permitted occupiers and could be removed at the whim of the Government or any policy change, the identical system practiced on all the Victorian Reserves. At the same time white men had legal access to the forests.

Echuca grew up on the red gum trade the *Riverine Herald* wrote, and during the past twenty-five years the forests on the Victorian side of the Murray had been stripped bare.

When Shadrach James was at Maloga, Matthews had made sure the tribesmen relaxed from their daily ritual and now at Cumeroogunga Shadrach realized the wisdom of that habit. He carried on the same idea and the men maintained their high standard of sport. As cricket was popular an invitation was sent to the Wamboota Cricket Team from the Cumeroogunga Club during the 1890 season.

The January sun was shimmering hot when the Wamboota Team arrived at the Moira platform where they were met by several Cumeroogunga men. They travelled the fourteen miles to the settlement in the station cart driven by one of the home team which was an experience no-one would forget. '… If the ribbons had not been handled by a competent man there would have been an accident,' declared a Wanamboota man.

After their dusty, bumpy ride, holding on as best they could with one hand and keeping the flies and dust away from their faces with the other, the Wamboot Team was in no fit shape to play cricket. They were taken to the school house where they met and talked with the Cumeroogunga residents and some of the white community from the Moama village to watch the cricket match. After they heard the day's planned events, and the river looking cool and inviting. They made for the river as soon as they could. One of the swimmers commented, 'Some of the dark people went, too, and demonstrated some wonderful aquatic feats.'

Refreshed, clean and happy the visitors from Moama accepted Shadrach's invitation to attend a meeting in the Mission House where they listened to the Aborigines singing a number of sacred songs and reciting a few prayers. 'We thoroughly enjoyed the meeting and learned that the Cumeroogunga people were not only good at wielding the bat and trundling the ball but possess higher traits of character.'

After the first round of cricket it was time to cool off again so they all went to the river with the villagers. They watched the Atkinson brothers, John and Edgar, spearing fish. Edgar was first in the water and with his spear in hand disappeared for quite a length of time before he resurfaced with a fish. He repeated his performance with his brother joining him and 'their agility in the water was marvellous.'[1]

The Wamboota men lost the match. The fielding and bowling of the Cumeroogunga Team was excellent and during the following cricket season, the Aboriginal cricketers' names appeared regularly in the newspapers. The white community often met such men as John and Edgar Atkinson, Alf and Bagot Morgan, Sampson Barber, Martin Simpson, Charlie Jackson, Jack Anderson, Jack Cooper, George and Willie Charles and Hughie Anderson.

It was acknowledged that the station men were excellent farmers. They worked hard and were rewarded with successful crops but, as usual, the rumblings made by those white men wishing to have the use of the property became loud and demanding. The much disliked George Bellenger resigned and the farm overseer, Bruce Ferguson, took over in 1893 and conditions on the station improved for a while.

The average population on Cumeroogunga was 170. A log hut was especially built for the elderly men and over a period of time more cottages appeared. A 3000-gallon tank was erected on a stand for the main water supply. The younger and healthy men cleared 500 acres of suckers and burnt off dead timber and the 'farm blocks men' ploughed seventy acres of land for wheat.[2]

Robert Cooper ploughed his own ten acres and set the wheat. John Atkinson had a return of wheat, although four acres of his twenty-seven had been destroyed by the rabbit plague. He cut seventeen acres for hay with a total yield of four tons, and the remaining six acres were stripped, producing seventy-two bushels. Because the station supplied him with twelve bags of wheat for seed he returned the same number, the balance being his own. He cut most of the hay into chaff and sold over one ton.[3]

Before the turn of the century twenty blocks on the reserve were being cultivated by the men and had there been more land available for farming that, too, would have been worked by eager residents hopefully waiting for a few acres. The station ran 160 sheep, thirty-two head of cattle and fifteen horses, all in good condition. There were twenty-nine cottages, all built by the men for their families. Some had timber floors and all were lined and whitewashed. The men provided the timber and the Board supplied the nails and iron.[4]

Sporting activities continued, including Cumeroogunga's own Football Club. Work in the village was a co-operative affair and the avenue of ornamental trees and the formation of guttered streets were rewarding projects. The sixty children received their education under Shadrach James and he had complete control of them. ' … If they did not turn up at school he would go out and get them and, if necessary, he would give them a spanking but nobody took exception to that.'[5]

Matthews and his wife tirelessly followed his resolve to support the Aborigines in their attempt to cope with the white authority which ruled their lives, inside and outside the reserves. Before the end of 1899 the couple had left Maloga and investigated the plight of Aborigines in South Australia where Janet began a mission at Mannum while Matthews attended to missionary work in Melbourne.

During the last year of the 1890s, five Cumeroogunga people died. Over the border of the Murray River some of their relations were named in the death list of twenty-six Aborigines in Victoria.

Chapter Thirteen

Farming, the Highs and the Lows 1900–1908

Daniel Matthews died at Mannum in1902 after a lifetime of ardently supporting a theory he applied to the aboriginal population of Australia, '… the poor remnant of the original owners … should be dealt with kindly, wisely and generously.'[1]

The Act to constitute the Commonwealth of Australia was proclaimed in Melbourne on 17 September 1900. Eight months later the Duke of York opened the first Commonwealth Parliament. The Exhibition Building was used for the ceremony as Parliament House would not hold the officials and celebrating crowds. Although the economic crisis of the 1900s resulted in a higher rate of unemployment in Victoria than anywhere else in Australia, a drop in population as families moved to other states, more than 12000 people enjoyed the opening of Parliament. The Melbourne Argus wrote of the crowd ' … free people, hopeful people, courageous people, entrusted with the working out of their own destiny and rejoicing in their liberty …'[1] Amongst those were the 'liberated' Aboriginal Victorians.

At Cumeroogunga the residents had increased to 200 and most were happy and comfortable. There were now thirty-two cottages, all with vegetable and flower gardens, their owners making good use of the water connected to each cottage. The farmers stripped 320 bags of wheat but the dry spring weather effected existing crops. The men worked outside the station and earned enough to pay 400 pounds for goods they ordered from Sydney.

In the following year the blocks were ruined, the result of the near drought conditions. Horses and cattle died and the rabbits thrived, and again the men had to seek work off the reserve. Some were employed as shearers, others as general farmhands.

Those who remained at Cumeroogunga made a living by fishing and sending their catch to Melbourne.

In 1902 the general health was reported as good, due mainly to the sanitary arrangements and regular visits of the medical officer. Even so there were seven deaths in a period of nine weeks and they all died of pneumonia.[2]

Daniel Matthews died this year at Mannum after a lifetime of ardently supporting a theory he applied to the aboriginal population of Australia, '… the poor remnant of the original owners … should be dealt with kindly, wisely and generously.'

The men repeatedly asked for blocks of land to farm as their own but there was no chance of this happening. Parliamentary Papers reveal that 'large blocks of the public estate were now being alienated to private owners, some of whom will probably debar Aborigines from hunting thereon.'[3]

When seasonal work was unavailable for the men who did not have the blocks at Cumeroogunga, they worked there building the stables, cottages, a buggy house and harness room, cutting pickets and making fences and gates. During the dry of 1902 and 1903 the manager encouraged the men to find employment away from the station as the fishing was poor, there was no bird life on the lakes, and the rabbits were diseased. Several of the 'block farmers' let their land to Indian hawkers for agistment as a source of finance but this was stopped by the manager.

Trouble was brewing again and some of the residents wrote to the Board but their suggestions were brushed aside. They were informed that any future complaints of a frivolous character would be severely dealt with but later a Board member did point out where improvements could be made and his recommendations were adopted.[4]

None of the parents liked the policy of sending their thirteen year old children from Cumeroogunga to work for people they did not know. When they spoke of their worries the Protection Board said every care was taken when the young girls and boys were apprenticed to white families. The Board was approached by the New South Wales Aboriginal Mission and asked if there would be any objection if they were to place the girls in homes. The offer was gladly accepted.

Several of the young men at Cumeroogunga wished to be apprenticed to the mechanical trades in Sydney. Inquiries were made in the larger towns in the surrounding district. Unfortunately without result.[5] The Board did not want youths living permanently on the reserve so they were sent out to work as farmhands to the white station owners. Some of the young boys were not paid for their labour.

Wheat crops were wiped out by a caterpillar plague in 1904 and once more the men and the women worked for their white neighbours nearby, and far away across the plains. It was about this time the Moona Cullah Mission came into being about twenty miles north-west of Deniliquin. Many of the tribal people were Wamba Wamba, and the mission was in their territory that extended over both sides of the Murray and into the plains. Tribespeople from the Edwards River and elsewhere were forced into close contact on the mission causing conflict and fear. Some made their way to Cumeroogunga and swelled that population to 260.

With the expectation of increased production, a farm supervisor was appointed to the station. The land had to be cleared of rabbits and the men dug, fumigated, hunted and trapped. They cleared and fenced paddocks, subdivided the greater part of the station and constructed eight miles of wire fencing. The station boundary was almost eight miles of a rabbit-proof fence, said to be the best in the district.

Soon there were 250 acres under wheat and 240 acres under oats. Two shorthorn pedigree bulls were bought to improve the stock; the cattle increased to 154 and 223 sheep grazed on the land. Cumeroogunga was looked upon as a model farming project.

Rain fell while wheat stripping was in progress and spoiled the yield. In the hot and dry season of 1907 and 1908 patches of pasture died and stock had to be sent to outside properties but it was reported that Cumeroogunga was holding out against the bad conditions.[6]

The men who had the use of the farm blocks turned to trapping fish and game to sell. They received good prices in Melbourne. Others had droving contracts taking cattle inland and returning with sheep. With weather improvement allowing, the men worked their own blocks as well as the station farm where government stock was run. They set up five water tanks in the paddocks that did not front the river and this meant that during the driest seasons the cattle could be watered. Previously they were driven to the river. The fruit trees and crops improved and the station farm and blocks produced a living for the families. The whole reserve was a paying concern.

The men commenced the grubbing of a lane of sixty chains out to the Barmah Road. When they finished the job it was a clear road to the township of Moama from Cumeroogunga.

Then came the announcement from the Board that brought about lasting changes to the lives of the aborigines at Cumeroogunga. It was decided to abolish the farm block system. ' … the residents of the station had, after sufficient opportunity, failed to properly work the blocks of land placed at their disposal … '. The Government proposed to work the land for the general benefit of the station and to pay the employed Aborigines wages on the usual scale.[7]

The land, cleared and cultivated by the Aboriginal men was claimed by the Board, and the report read, '… the resumption of farm blocks caused disappointment to some …'[8]

Chapter Fourteen

The Act that Broke Hearts and Homes 1909–1937

New South Wales introduced that State's first Aborigines Protection Act in 1909. Administered by the Aborigines Welfare Board, it meant the control of the full-blood and part-Aboriginal people was in the hands of Government.

As it happened, over a long period of time, a local committee group had 'kept an eye' on the residents of Cumeroogunga, their homes, and the station. The activities of this committee had been one of the grievances expressed by the Aborigines of Cumeroogunga to the Board. The Act made provision for the committee to carry on its 'duty' in spite of the objections made by the Aboriginal people. The local members of the committee were of some importance in the community and usually included one member of the police force.

After the men lost their blocks a drought followed and lasted three years bringing with it the expected problems and by 1913 flood banks had to be built to protect the village and crops. During the floods thousands of rabbits were killed and their skins sold.

The children kept their school grounds weeded and tidy and helped to keep the garden in front of their school free of weeds. They were spoken of as obedient and courteous children, tidy and clean. But some of those same children were taken suddenly away from all they knew and loved and deposited in a far off home as servants or sent away to take up an apprenticeship. They became 'wards.' If a girl or boy ran away from their place of employment, the Aborigines Welfare Board had the power to have them arrested.

The Board could control the employment of the adults; could have employment terminated; could direct wages into the charge of the Superintendent of the Aborigines Welfare. These full blood Aboriginal people were prohibited from any permanent association with non-Aboriginal persons. Life under the Act, and the steady replacement of white managers at Cumeroogunga bred resentment, caused great unhappiness, and increased unrest amongst the people. An amendment to the Act in 1915 was designed with a view to the effective administration of a policy dealing with Aboriginal children.[1]

The Act brought a woman onto the scene at Cumeroogunga with a title that brought chills to the hearts of all at the station. She was the Home Finder. A well organized plan was put into action to take the lighter coloured children from their families, or in some cases where there were no parents, from their relatives and friends. During this one year the Home Finder descended on Cumeroogunga and Warangesda four times. The chosen girls were taken from their homes and travelled under escort to Cootamundra, north-east of Wagga Wagga, They were placed in a general form of a training home with the name of Cootamundra House.[2]

Being so far from their homes it was impossible for them to have visits from their parents and families. The name of Cootamundra House was seared for ever into the minds of all the young women and their families. The Wiradjuri word, *cootamundry*, described a place for turtles and marshlands. The district of Cootamundry was settled in the 1830s and by the 1860s the village was planned.

A couple of years later there were proud proclamations that Cumeroogunga Station was one of the largest under the Board's control and a special effort was made, not only to make it self-supporting, but to show a handsome profit in connection with farming and stock raising operations. White visitors to the reserve were taken along the three streets in the village where they admired the sixty buildings which included forty-six cottages. They strolled through the orchard, and they praised the vegetable gardens.[3]

The Government decided the local committee who had access to the residents' homes had, after all, been an unsuccessful venture. Two Inspectors of the Aborigines Welfare Board were appointed instead.

The young girls and boys were systematically removed from the station to be trained as housemaids and apprentices. By 1919 they were being taken by force. When the residents knew the police and officers were coming to the station parents concealed their children. Some hid beneath the school but were often found and dragged out screaming. Others scattered to the trees and the river. Families were callously separated.

The cottages no longer housed happy, singing people. The plan was to lower the numbers on the reserve by assimilating as many young people as possible into the general community. Thomas Shadrach James knew the sorrow caused by the government experiments and the experiences which affected his pupils and their families. He retired in 1921 and the people were without his kind support.

During the 1920s the girls taken from Cumeroogunga attended the school at Cootamundra House. The older young women were trained for domestic service. By 1927 the Board asserted the Home continued to be one of the most satisfactory features of the Board's activities. The average number of inmates for the years was forty-two. When the girls left to take up satisfactory positions they were kept under observation of a lady officer appointed for the purpose.[4]

The boys were taken to Kempsey and installed at the Aboriginal Boys Training Home north of Port Macquarie.

Houses promised by the Board to replace the deteriorating cottages the men built with pride years earlier, were just not appearing and many families were living in bark shelters. The Aborigines were in such a situation that if they complained too loudly or too often they were in danger of losing rations, expulsion from the station or the removal of their children. If the manager or the Inspector of Aborigines were unsympathetic listeners, these were likely punishments. There was a real danger if the manager had a set on any one person or family as he had the full approval of the authorities to expel those he chose. Police officers were expected to co-operate with the manager.

During the years since the takeover of the farm blocks the men were left with little dignity when they were paid for reserve work with rations and sometimes a small wage. Conditions were even worse when some managers favored their bullets and batons. 5

The years passed going from bad to worse. There was very little finance with a staff of untrained white people. There were no agricultural opportunities for the men and boys, and no training for the women. There was no future for the girls other than as a maid for a white family. In desperation some families left Cumeroogunga to find homes and work. The manager quickly destroyed twenty-one of the houses.

One of the young girls at the station was suspected of having tuberculosis. She was ill and it was arranged for her to be taken to Deniliquin Hospital for X-rays in the station truck. As members of the staff were the only people allowed to ride in the cabin the patient was placed in the back of the three-ton truck. It was a bitterly cold winter morning. After the child's ride of forty-five miles, she was diagnosed as consumptive. By 1934 the number of sick people escalated alarmingly. Eye diseases were common, and so was the lack of food for families.

Another new manager arrived at the station named Danvers. He was impressed with the residents and reported they were more sophisticated than those elsewhere on stations. He praised Shadrach's teaching and said some of the older men and women could write 'just like copperplate.'[6]

He knew thousands of pounds had been spent over the years on the Cumeroogunga Reserve but he found the land overgrown and covered with burrs; rabbits infested the whole station; fences were down; houses in a dilapidated state. One of the farming men told Danvers the previous manager would not allow them to work on the farm. When he said he needed food for his family and was willing to work for rations Danvers spoke with the station men and was told they all wanted to work on the farm. Clearing and cleaning the reserve land commenced.

If the state of the farm set in the 2,800 acres was a surprise and disappointment to Danvers what could have been his reaction to the degraded and hapless Aborigines existing at Cumeroogunga? There were twenty-five weatherboard cottages, without baths, and 172 people. He told the Board the residents bathed in the river. Most of the cottages had flour bag lined walls and no flooring. As there were few beds most children slept on the ground with only a blanket. About 113 people lived in twenty canvas dwellings. There were no cooking utensils.

Malnutrition was obvious to Danvers, and so were the children and adults suffering with the eye disease trachoma which left untreated, often caused blindness.

He discovered the camp on the Victorian side of the river where expelled people lived and was informed they preferred that to being under the control of the Board at Cumeroogunga. Sometimes there were from twenty-four to forty people.[7]

Danvers reported his findings to the Board. '… Down on the river bank of the river there were about a dozen bag huts with no floor in them. I have been down there on a wet day and have seen children lying on the earth floors. I have seen people lying on the floors with one blanket between them …'[8]

One of the final crushing blows delivered to the Cumeroogunga people was when the Board leased 2000 acres of the 2800 acres of the Reserve land which they had always considered their own. It went to a white farmer to graze his sheep and mill the timber. He employed several of the Aboriginal station men but paid them, 'only a few shillings.'

While the residents waited for their new houses the timber from the reserve was cut and sold. Lavatories were urgently needed in the settlement and nine were built. They were sent to the Aboriginal Reserve at Balranald, 120 miles away.

At a time when Danvers was in charge of 250 to 300 people on the station, a double certificate nurse took up duties and she treated seventy people per day for eye infections. The food supplies were still inadequate and before the men could leave the station to find a paying job they were compelled to report to the manager.

Chapter Fifteen

Cumeroogunga's Rebellion 1838–1840

Evidence was gathered regarding the Aborigines of New South Wales who were tucked away on remote reserves. Facts were clearly shown of the apathetic approach maintained towards them, the mis-management and their ill-treatment.

At Cumeroogunga in 1838 there were 248 Aboriginal residents and a white staff of fourteen. There was little need for the farm machinery with the larger part of the reserve leased to the white private individual which, an officer of the Public Service Board commented, could be regarded 'only as unsatisfactory conditions.'[1]

Some of the Aboriginal men had lived and worked on the station for twenty and thirty years with wives and children. It hurt them to see their land leased to a non-Aborginal, and a lot of the farm machinery being sent to other reserves. Anything that was left was mostly broken or worn out and useless. The water supply system had broken down and remained that way as the station stock was sold.

Any of the happy, prosperous years the people had lived through were a memory and the prospect of a similar future died before it began. About half the number of residents lived in huts of hessian and bark. The surviving cottages, usually with two rooms, were overcrowded, badly ventilated and in need of repair.

On 4 February 1939 the Cumeroogunga people acted in defiance of their manager and the Rules and Regulations they were expected to obey. All but four families walked off the reserve and crossed the Murray River into Victoria's Barmah.[2]

The Melbourne Herald declared the walkout from the Cumeroogunga Aboriginal Reserve was a protest against the existing conditions. The Aboriginal people expressed their disgust by asking for the removal of the manager, Mr. McQuiggan.[3]

In a letter to the Government a request was made for an independent inquiry as well as McQuiggan's dismissal. The public learned the living quarters on the river bank were made of hessian bags, boughs and bark. The press told Victoria the rebels believed they would be better off living on a Victorian Government sustenance than the daily three shilling and sixpence ration allowance for adults and five pence per child.

The few short articles that appeared in the Melbourne newspapers about the 'walkout' were outshone by the interest taken in Britain where the new deep bomb-proof shelters were being planned. The Melbourne theatre goers were coaxed by large advertisement to see the current films which were bringing in the crowds, 'Marie Antoinette' and Pygmalion.'

Nevertheless, some men were stirred by the significance of the Rebellion on the Murray. The Honorary Secretary of the Anthropological Society of Victoria, Mr A. Rosenblum, believed the white community, as well as the Aborigines, needed education. 'The really important thing is to educate the whites to the fact that the native is an intelligent being capable of receiving education.'

He applauded the projected raising of the status of Aborigines by the Federal Government in its new policy which advocated the establishment of Patrol Officers and the provision of medical educational services. Rosenblum declared confidently if the new regulations were carried out in their entirety it was unlikely there would be any further complaints from anthropologists about the treatment of the Aborigines.[4]

Father Ernst Wurms, Director of the Catholic Pallottine Mission College described the new policy as, '… the first bright spot in the development of native laws.' As a priest and anthropologist he had worked for eight years with the Aborigines in the north-west of Australia.[5]

The families from Cumeroogunga had been living in the Victorian river camp for a fortnight without any acknowledgement of their letter to the government. The Melbourne Herald announced triumphantly that the people were 'still holding out' and were determined not to cross the river into New South Wales in spite of the fact that food was in such short supply. It was generally believed that if the Government realized the people were in earnest their requests would be granted.[6]

The Melbourne Aborigines League sent money to Barmah to help support the families while their cause waited for some recognition. During the summer and autumn months of hardship and anxiety their determination kept them going. As they moved into the winter months the League again sent money to ease the shortage of food. There was never enough food or milk and it was impossible to keep the rain out of the shelters. The floors were sloppy with mud and the blankets were wet.

Without fruit and vegetables for the children, the rain and cold weather, the adults concern forced a large number to return to the Station. They found they were victimized. Seventy-seven people returned to the river camp. Of that number thirty-three were children, some were babies.

Victorian Government authorities were reluctant to be involved as the people belonged to the New South Wales Aboriginal Reserve. However, some were lucky enough to be given some government sustenance.

As there were twenty-nine children of school age in the camp, a deputation of the people approached the Minister of Education in Melbourne with regard to a school for their children in Barmah. It was considered by the authority that the children should be attending the Cumeroogunga school every day which was over the river and two miles from the camp. A few campers received government assistance but that would be terminated in October which would drive most of the families back to the reserve.[7]

They were still on the river in September hopeful that their voices would be heard. The voice that was heard loud and clear was that of the Prime Minister of Australia, Robert Menzies, on 3 September 1939: 'It is my melancholy duty to inform you officially that in consequence of the persistence by Germany in her invasion of Poland, Great Britain has declared war on her, and that, as a result, Australia is also at war.'

During 1939, three Aboriginal people were chosen to contest the next State elections in New South Wales. One was Mrs Pearl Gibb with an effort to unseat the Chief Secretary, because, 'he has denied Aborigines the right to direct representation on the Aborigines Protection Board.'[8]

With the advent of war many of the Aboriginal men were called up for civil construction work and others volunteered for war service. The Public Service Board released the Report and Recommendations in 1940 when the families were back on Cumeroogunga:

> To improve and change the circumstances under which the Aborigines exist in Australia; the Aborigines Welfare Board to be reorganized; the system of Homes for young boys and girls to be examined; workers on reserves to be paid in money instead of rations; schools to have qualified teachers and not to use the managers as tutors.[9]

Included in the recommendations for Cumeroogunga were glass windows in the cottages for light and ventilation; cooking and eating utensils provided with delay. Houses were to be built and planned to give more privacy. There would be land enough for the occupiers to have gardens and poultry. Aboriginal men would be employed in place of white contractors.[10]

There would be efforts made to assimilate the increasing part-Aboriginal people into the general community. One of the regulations was: The right of the managers must be retained to order a person off a station, and to also expel.[11]

Chapter Sixteen

This Land is My Mother 1980s

John Atkinson, a Yotti Yotta man

John (Sandy) Atkinson was one of the very puzzled children who camped with their families on the bank of the Murray River in 1839, too young to understand the reason why he had left his home at Cumeroogunga:

'If you could think of yourself coming here, even 500 years ago, you would have found a fascinating man, and if you'd had the opportunity to study than man you would have found his life was built around the land itself. Had you heard him say to you, 'This land is my mother. This land, my mother, will not see me die of thirst or hunger, and when I lay down to sleep with my head on the bare ground because that is my mother's breast,' you could perhaps begin to understand the link. That man could not leave the land where he was born and where his people had spent thousands of years. He was a very, very confident man who knew his own country and lived in it. I think you have to get a picture first in your mind to fully appreciate the tremendous hold the land had on our people.

'My people were born and raised at Cumeroogunga, and their people came from Maloga where the traditional tribe actually congregated. I was born and raised at Cumeroogunga. When I was a very small boy there were lots of people living there and it was a very big Mission with streets, and the people worked there. They even had their own cattle.

'If you can imagine what a dramatic effect that mass walk-off had on those people. Fresh in the memories of the older ones was the traditional living, and from that to Cumeroogunga. Those people crossed the river from a base that had become their home, although traditionally the land was theirs. They were fighting for better conditions on the place and to prove their point I guess there was nothing else to do but walk off and hope to draw attention of outside people to their trouble. They had to do something. It was a do or die thing.

'The manager of Cumeroogunga was the boss man and the Government was not sympathetic. They held all the aces. The Cumeroogunga people lived under a handout system. It wasn't one they liked very much but it was the only thing they had. Sheep and cattle had eaten the food that their food (native animals) used to eat, so the Aboriginal people were there on the reserve, by force and circumstance.

'Those men knew they were in for one hell of a time if they moved away from that handout. Over the river there would be no system like that. Well, they did go, and they took their families with them, and many a day was spent hunting duck and getting some fish, anything that was about that they could get to feed the people.

'Another important thing to consider was the effect this all had on the women and kids. I guess in those times they did not understand politics and when things happened, they got drawn in whether they liked it or not. There are stories told, even today, how the children sat along the bank of the river every evening before it got dark, just looking across at their homes on the other side, and crying to go back. They didn't know why they could not just dive in and swim across that water to their homes. They were that close.

'To us, Cumeroogunga was home. We went to church there and to school. It was written in the manager's manual, quite clearly, that all I needed was the third grade education, and that's all I ever had. Most of the people of my time, and before me, had the same education. I'm sure I got a lot of strength and inspiration from my parents that gave me the great start in my life. Dad seemed to have a way of life that I would like to follow. Never too interested in alcohol, he seemed so intent on raising a good family and, with Mum; their time was devoted to us. Nine boys and one girl. Those days I'm sure were very hard for them. Church and Sunday school played a large part in my life, too.

'Our education at Cumeroogunga was poor, but out there was our home. It still is to some of our people of course. A long time back, the Government should have done the honourable thing by saying, 'Right, there are the deeds to your land and now you are in complete control. You tell us what you need to do here and we will support you. The responsibility is yours. If you fail you are in big trouble.' That would have worked I'm sure because now you would have had people who grew up with that system. But instead of that they kept the title. You see, you don't own anything. Nothing is yours. So you don't have the same personal community involvement. The longer we went at Cumeroogunga the worse it got.

'The story of Cumeroogunga is not a happy one. If you take into account all the years the people were held down. For instance, that white man who had land given to him on Cumeroogunga for his own use by the Government. The Aboriginal people were ignored about it when they wanted it. He built an empire almost, on the reserve. There was the white man who leased land and treated our people like mud. Once one of these men ran a channel straight up through the centre of the Mission and pumped water. One time the people asked him could some be pumped for their land and the white fellow said they'd have to pay for it. He set a ridiculous price. They pulled the same rank on him, and told him if he wanted the water he'd have to pay them.

'You know, the tribal people made yards in the river with boughs, usually after floods. These fish got caught in the bough yards, as they called them, when they came back into the forest. These fish traps have long gone. Steamboats and timber workers cleared them away long ago. Still, we know where the tribal people had them and where their many campsites were in the forests and along the river. We know where the canoe trees are and the middens.

'One of the things I've found a help in life is never let anyone else see that you are in any way upset about things. Aboriginal people should be very good at that. They've done it for thousands and thousands of years. Always been so calm about solving their problems. I always remember something that was told to me by an old man at Cumeroogunga when I was a little boy:

'Always be like a duck on top – calm, cool and collected. Underneath – paddle like hell!

Notes

Chapter 5: Occupation and Contact

1. Manning Clark, foreword., An emigrant Mechanic; Settles and Convicts, first published in London in 1847; reprint 1852, Melbourne University Press, 1969
2. Reverend John Bulmer, 1887, Some Account of the Aborigines of the Lower Murray, Wimmera, Gippsland and Maneroo, Mission Society, Melbourne
3. Riverine Herald, September 1865
4. A. Pioneer, *Reminescences of Australian Life*
5. Reverend John Bulmer, 1887
6. Alan Goss, *Charles Joseph La Trobe*, Melbourne University Press 1980
7. New South Wales Votes and Proceedings Legislative Council, 1843
8. La Trobe Letter Book, 24 February 1843, La Trobe Collection, State Library of Victoria
9. Harley D.W. Forster, ed. 1965, E. M. Curr, *Recollections of Squatting in Victoria*, Melbourne University Press
10. E. M. Curr
11. Reverend R. J. Merewether, *Diary of a Working Clergyman*, London 1854
12. Daniel Matthews, *Journal and Proceedings of the Royal Society of New South Wales*, 1889

Chapter 6: The Meeting of the Waters

1. Reverend John Bulmer, op.cit.
2. A. Morris, Rich River, Echuca, Victoria, 1952
3. ibid
4. A. Anderson, *Victoria: From discovery to Federation*, Rigby, Adelaide, 1974
5. Reverend John Bulmer, op.cit
6. John Atkinson, interview with Tess De Araugo
7. Reverend John Bulmer, op.cit
8. Miss Winifred Chauncy, interview with Tess De Araugo
9. R. V. Billis and A. S. Kenyan, *Pastoral Pioneers of Port*

Phillip, Stockland Press, Melbourne, 1974

10. *Riverine Herald*, December 1863
11. ibid, February 1863
12. ibid, July 1863
13. Ernest Michael Kelsall, interview with Tess De Araugo
14. *Riverine Herald*, July 1863
15. Ibid
16. Ibid, October 1863

Chapter 7: Corroboree at Moama

1 Reverend John Bulmer, op.cit

2 Ibid

3 John Atkinson, interview with Tess De Araugo

4 *Riverine Herald*, January 1864

5 Report of the Central Board Appointed to Watch over the Interests of the Aborigines in the Colony of Victoria, La Trobe Collection, State Library of Victoria

6 C. E. Strutt, Report of the Select Committee, Victorian Legislative Council, Votes and Proceedings, 1858–1859

7 Daniel Matthews, *op.cit.*, vols. 1V–V

8 Report of the New South Wales Aboriginal Protection Association, 1881, *New South Wales Votes and Proceedings*, Vol. 3, 1883

9 Riverine Herald, March l867

Chapter 8: Prosperity and Poverty

1 *Riverine Herald*, April 1865

2 Ibid, November

3 A. Morris, *River Transport on the Greater Murray Network*, Royal Historical Society of Victoria, Victorian Historical Magazine, Vol. 44, 1973

4 Manning Clark, *Sources of Australian History*, Oxford Press, 1960

5 Manning Clark, A Short History of Australia, Tudor Distributors, Sydney, 1961

6 ibid

7 M. Cannon, *Life in the Country*, Thomas Nelson, Victoria,

1973

8 Manning Clark, A Short …

9 D. Pike, general ed., *Australian Dictionary of Biography*, Melbourne University Press,

10 P. Kin, EF. Fosberyi, *New South Wales Votes and Proceedings*, Legislative Assembly , 1883

11 *Riverine Herald*, April 1866

12 Ibid, January 1867

13 Ibid, March 1867

14 Daniel Matthews, *Native Tribes …*

15 A. B. Peirce, *Knocking About*, Facsimile Edition, Shoestring Press, Wangaratta, 1984

Chapter 9: A Changing, Shrinking World

1 P. Phillips, *River Boat Days on the Murray, Darling and Murrumbidgge*, Lansdown Press, Melbourne, 1972

2 ibid

3 ibid

4 Daniel Matthews, *Native Tribes …*

5 Ibid

6 D. Pike, op.cit

7 Ibid

8 *New South Parliamentary Debates*, 1884

9 E. Docker, *Simply Human Beings*, Jacaranda Press, Melbourne, 1964

10 C. E. Rowley, *Outcasts in White Australia*, Pelican Books, 1972

11 Report of the Aborigines Protection Association, 30 June 1881, *New South Wales Votes and Proceedings*, Vol. 3

12 Daniel Matthews, *Native Tribes … op.cit*

13 ibid

14 ibid

Chapter 10: Maloga the Mission

1 Cuthbert Fetherstonhaugh, *After Many Days*, E. F. W. Cole, Melbourne

2 Daniel Matthews, op.cit

3 E. W. Palmer, *Deniliquin Chronicle and Riverine Gazette*, May 1880

4 Ibid

5 *Riverine Herald*, June 1864, The Murray Revisited

6 Daniel Matthews, op.cit

7 *New South Wales Votes and Proceedings*, Vol. 3, 1883

8 Reverend J. Gribble, *Black But Comely: Aboriginal life in Australia*, London

9 *New South Wales Votes and Proceedings*, Vol. 3, 1883

10 A. Jackomos, *Thomas Shadrach James, 1856–1945*, Identity, January 1979

11 Greg James, interview with Tess De Araugo

12 L. Fox, *The Struggle for Dignity*, Melbourne, 1962

13 Report, New South Wales Legislative Assembly, 1883

14 *New South Wales Parliamentary Debates*, 1883

15 Daniel Matthews, op.cit

16 Central Board to Watch over the Aborigines, Secretary, Outward Correspondence, B329, 1883, Australian Archives, Brighton

17 D. Pike, op.cit

18 Greg James, op.cit

19 Central Board to Watch over the Aborigines, Secretary, Outward correspondence, B329, 1885, Australian Archives, Brighton

20 *New South Wales Votes and Proceedings Legislative Assembly*, Vol. 2, 1886

21 Central Board, op.cit. Secretary, Outward Corresponndence, B329, 1887

Chapter 11: Cumeroogunga a Prelude

1 New South Wales Legislative Assembly 1889

2 ibid

3 ibid

4 ibid

5 Nancy Cato, *Mister Maloga*, University of Queensland Press, 1976

6 New South Wales Legislative Assembly 1889

7 Ibid

8 Ibid 1890

9 Ibid 1891

10 Central Board, secretary, Outward Correspondence, B329, 1890, Australian Archives, Brighton,

Chapter 12: Cumeroogunga Farmers

1 *Riverine Herald*, March 1890

2 *New South Wales Votes and Proceedings*, Legislative Assembly, 1894

3 Ibid

4 Ibid, 1899

5 *New South Wales Parliamentary Papers*, Evidence Before a Select Committee, Vol. 6, 1937-1938

Chapter 13: Farming – the Highs and the Low

1 M. Barnard, *A History of Australia*, Angus and Robertson 1980

2 *New South Wales Parliamentary Papers*, Votes and Proceedings, Vol 3, 1903

3 ibid, 1904

4 ibid

5 ibid, 1905

6 ibid, 1908

7 ibid

8 ibid, 1909

Chapter 14: The Act that Broke Hearts and Homes

1 *New South Wales Parliamentary Papers*, Votes and Proceedings, 1916

2 ibid

3 ibid

4 ibid, Vol. 1. 1928

5 L. Fox, op.cit

6 *New South Wales Parliamentary Papers*, Report and Recommendations of the Public Service Board, Vol. 5, 1937–1938

7 ibid
8 ibid

Chapter 15: Cumeroogunga's Rebellion

1 *New South Wales Parliamentary Papers*, Report and Recommendations of the Public Service Board, Vol. 7, 1940
2 C. D. Rowley, op.cit.
3 *Melbourne Herald*, February, 1939
4 ibid
5 ibid
6 ibid
7 ibid, October, 1939
8 ibid, March, 1939
9 *New South Wales Parliamentary Papers*, Report and Recommendations , op.cit.
10 ibid
11 ibid

Chapter 16: This Land is My Mother: 1980s

1 Interview with the author.

Part Two

The Heart of It All

Preface

When Daniel Matthews wrote of the period prior to the formation of his Maloga Mission he knew many of the young girls had already been victims of the white men's lust. He, and others, had seen the wine shanty at John O'Shanassy's Moira Station where the employees drank and danced at night not far from the natives' camp. It was easy for the station men to ply the girls with wine. O'Shanassy migrated to Port Phillip in 1839 and later was elected to the Victorian Legislative Council. He was a founder of the Colonial Bank of Australasia Victoria.

Matthews visited the isolated Aboriginal camps in the forests, along the waterways, in the sand-hills, and on the settlers' stations which were comprised of tens of thousands of acres where the tribesmen were used as cheap labourers and some of the women as sex partners.

The age of the women was no barrier to white men, especially the group of drunken sawyers who descended on a Yotti Yotta tribesman and his wife in their mia-mia on the outskirts of the Barmah Forest. They terrorized the couple. When the tribesman defended his wife the men hit and punched him into unconsciousness. After they had raped the woman they heated an iron in the campfire and burned her with it. Still their warped minds were not satisfied. They kicked the tortured woman to death. Sometime later three men were charged with the woman's murder but they were not found guilty.

Matthews rode many times to O'Shanassy's to persuade the young women to go with him to Maloga but their parents were told at the station that Matthews intended to take all the children away, that he would ill-treat them. He persisted until he had collected a number of young mothers aged thirteen and fourteen and their babies. They were soon joined by mothers and pregnant girls from different Aboriginal groups.

The white fathers remained protected from the law although their identity was often known to Matthews and the Aboriginal Protection Boards of Victoria and New South Wales. These fathers came from all walks of life. Some of the young mothers gave their babies the white father's surname, that parent who disowned his own child born to a tribal girl.

Many families who agreed to live at the Maloga Mission from 1874 were already bearing non-Aboriginal surnames. With the escalation of white occupation and its accompaniment of diseases and deaths, orphaned children were cared for by relations, or by surviving members of the same group and sometimes becoming in name part of a family although without blood relationship. Daniel and Janet Matthews knew some of the tribal people a few of whom were born before the occupation of their territories and their ages are guessed, or judged, by the Matthews. At Maloga some of the Old People were Old Gracie, Old Molly, Wild Kitty, Old Maria, Old Kitty, King Billy, Murray Jack, Old Micky, Old Edward Walker.

The first child Matthews cared for was tiny Jemima Burns. A little boy he took a great interest in was Bagot Morgan. There was Old Gracie's granddaughter, Sarah, fourteen years old, with her small son, Herbert, fifteen months old. (Sarah later married Old Fred Walker's son, Fred). Another young girl of fourteen was Lizzie Atkinson. She took her two year old son, Frankie, with her to the Mission. (Lizzie later married Sampson Barber).

Old Kitty had four children to a white man working in tribal country named Atkinson. Kitty's children were Johnny, Aaron, Eddie (Edgar) and Lizzie. Old Kitty had a second family to a white man named Cooper. Their names were Billy, Bobby, Jackie and Ada. (Ada later married Thomas Shadrach James).

Lizzie attended the school classes at Maloga. She wanted her mother to leave O'Shanassy's station where she lived in the camp with the younger Cooper children, and go to the Mission. Her brothers, Johnny, now twenty-six, and Aaron, twenty, were sheep branding for O'Shanassy at Moira. Old Kitty and her Cooper children moved to Maloga.

Government policies over the years shuffled the people between Aboriginal Reserves and Church Mission Stations as regulations and rules heaved in efforts to humour landowners and townspeople. The Aboriginal families were separated, expelled, and transferred from one reserve to another. Consequently, descendants of many tribes came together, inside and outside, the places still called Mission.

Thousands of Aboriginal descendants can trace their ancestry back to the tribal people who lived on their own land throughout the Murray Valley and beyond, and those who were buried on the Maloga Mission or in the Cumeroogunga Cemetery on the hill.

The descendants of some of these people have now breathed life into the statistics, the physical descriptions and names of so any I had become familiar with on paper, often through the heartrending letters they had written themselves to Government bodies, and the replies they received. For years I had felt, and shared, their anger, their grief, their frustrations, as I followed their life stories through the pages of government documentation, Mission and Church records, Aboriginal Station reports, journals of early settlers, newspaper files and those dozens of revealing letters.

Garry Briggs and Kevin Gardiner, house-builders for Jack O'Mullane of Echuca.

My brother, Jack O'Mullane, and his wife, Elaine, lived in Echuca and knew many Aboriginal people in the district. Several of the men were builders of their home. Jack and Elaine led me to

Paul Egan and his wife Alice at their home near the Campaspe in Echuca. Alice arranged for me to meet Mrs Louise Atkinson.

'Auntie Louie is the oldest Aboriginal lady in Echuca. She remembers people and places from the old days.'

I met Mrs Atkinson for the first time in 1983. She was seventy-five, and although she had recently had a stroke she was happy to talk to me about life, and people, on and off the Missions. She wanted her old friend, Auntie Ivy to share the hours of reminiscing with her as she, too had lived on the Missions as her parents had before she was born.

'Auntie Ivy, that's Mrs Sampson. She lives over the river at Barmah.'

The date was set by Alice for the visit but she was ill and had arranged for Jean Egan to take her place.

Chapter One

The Old Days

It was a cold, wet day in July 1983, when Mrs Louise Atkinson and her younger friend, Mrs Jean Egan, took me to meet Mrs Ivy Sampson. She lived by herself in her weatherboard cottage at Barmah, in Victoria, on the Murray River. She was eighty-four and totally blind. Prepared meals were brought to her and she had friends and relatives calling in every day. She was Auntie Ivy to them all.

She was sitting in a large, old, comfortable armchair in the lounge room in front of a warmly glowing fire, a walking stick beside her chair and logs within easy reach with which to stoke the fire. As she had not been forewarned of my visit, Mrs Atkinson spoke softly to her, placing her hand on one shoulder.

'I've brought someone to see you,' she whispered.

'I know that,' Ivy laughed. 'She wants to talk to me.'

Frail, silver hair framing her smiling face, Ivy Sampson held out both her hands to me and looked unseeingly into my face, waiting for me to speak. I took her thin, but large hands in mine and told her I would like to talk about the old days, and about as many people as she could remember. Her face lit up. She laughed, looked at Louie and back to me.

'Will you know who I'm talking about?'

I mentioned a few family names and spoke of the early experiences of the tribal people.

'Why do you want to know?'

I explained I was writing the Aboriginal History of Victoria and I needed to know more than I could find in official documents. Ivy Sampson patted my hand and agreed. She leaned back in her chair.

'Make a cup of tea, Louie. You'll find some cake in the tin.' She turned her head to me. 'We like to talk about the early days.'

While we had our tea and cake we spoke generally about the weather, the river, the Murray Cod, pensions, and the hospitals for the elderly – where Ivy Sampson definitely did not want to spend any time. As Jean Egan and I washed the dishes we knew Ivy and Louie were anxious to commence their trip into the days gone by. Louie told Ivy I had a tape recorder. Ivy was not concerned.

Ivy Sampson in her Barmah home during one of our talking sessions in 1983

'Can't see it,' she said briefly, so I gave it to her to hold. She ran her hands over the small recorder and after hearing a conversation played back, which delighted her, we were ready to begin our travel through time.

'My father was born in Dunolly in 1857. He was named Tom Dunolly and he was from the Loddon Tribe. He was only seven when he was taken to the Mission our people called the Blue Shirt Mission. I don't know why they had that name for it but the man who was in charge was called Parker.'

Edward Stone Parker was one of the five men appointed as Protectors of Aborigines. He arrived from England in 1839. He established the Mt Franklin Aboriginal Station and controlled it during 1841 to 1850. The school and station were not closed until the 1860s. In the 1970s my husband and I discovered one of our friends was the grandson of E.S. Parker.

'The little kids might have had to wear blue shirts,' Louie offered.

'Yes, they must have. The Mission was at Mt Franklin. When the school was closed they shifted them children to Coranderrk at Healesville.' Ivy raised her arm. 'He had a photo taken, my father did.' She felt for her stick and when she stood up she was surprisingly tall, even though slightly stooped. Ivy made her way to the buffet which she kept locked. She took a key from her cardigan pocket, moved her fingers over the drawer until she found the keyhole, unlocked it, and lifted out several well preserved large photographs.

Louise Atkinson with Ivy.

'My father,' Ivy said proudly as she held them up for me to see. They were of a very young, handsome, well dressed man. She locked the photographs away again and moved confidently back to her chair.

'All the people from there were collected up and taken to

Coranderrk. A lot got taken from here, too. Some children didn't have parents and some did. That made it hard for the young ones when they got older to know who they were; who their parents were. Some still don't know who they're from.'

There was silence in the room for fully half a minute, broken only by the crackles and movement of the burning fire.

'One time I was taken to that Mission of Parker's by a man from the Melbourne Museum when they had a get-together at Mt Franklin where them stones are. I could see then, you know. It was a big affair that day. Boomerang throwing and all sorts of things. I was there where all the Blackfellas are buried in the cemetery. And Parker's in the middle of them. Buried there right alongside the Blackfellas. I was glad that man took us. All the other white fellas are buried in a different part of the cemetery. There were others of us who had people that had gone to that Mission. My friend, Mary Short, was there too, and I can remember when her father, Old Alf Davis, would come to our place to see my father and I'd hear them talk about when they were at the Blue shirt Mission.'

In 1965 Ivy was one of the guests at the Centenary celebrations. She refers to Alan West, Curator of Anthropology. The Jajowurongs of the Loddon River knew the mountain as Lalgambook. The extinct volcano area near Daylesford was known as Jim Crow by the squatters.

In 1864 twelve adults and children belonging to the Jajowurong Tribe were taken from Mt Franklin to Coranderrk. Within twelve years, Tom Dunolly and Tom Farmer were the only survivors.

'Your mother was from the Goulburn wasn't she, Auntie Ivy?' Louie asked.

'Yes. My mother was Jessie Hamilton and she married my father in 1876 at the Coranderrk Station. She come from Seymour. They'd got her to that station too, when she a child.'

The Taungurong Tribe of 1000 was comprised of eight groups when the Goulburn River Protectorate was established north of Seymour in 1839. The Headman of the Nerbaluk, one of the eight groups, left the Goulburn with eighty tribesmen and arrived in Melbourne in 1839 having been incorrectly informed they would receive blankets and food from the new Governor. The Nerbaluk leader became known as Billy Hamilton by the Government administration after he had led his men against squatters on their tribal land in 1843. A white landholder was Billy Hamilton.

'My mother was forty by the time she had me in 1899,' Ivy said. 'She'd already had nine children and four of them, James, Lily, Jessie and William, had already died. Lily and Jessie both died at Coranderrk.' Ivy lay her head back on the armchair and closed her eyes.

'I was born at Barmah, here, on the ground by the river at Madowla – they called it Lower Moira, right across the river from the Maloga Mission.' She opened her eyes and leaned forward. 'My brother Tommy was seventeen years old then. The next was Willie, then fourteen year old Peter, and David. He was twelve. My sister, Sissy, was seven and Richard was three.'

Louie nodded. 'That time when they made a lot of the people leave their place on the Missions and go out, a lot of them people came here from Coranderrk,' Louie said. 'Sent them out of their houses.'

Ivy looked at me and nodded. 'With their children, too.' She directed her nodding head towards Louie. 'This one's people did.'

'That's the Briggs,' Louie added for my benefit.

'Yes. Others come too, and some of them settled on Maloga and some camped down on the opposite side of the Murray where my mother and father had their place in Victoria. He bought a piece of ground and he worked hard to get it. He made a bark hut. He stripped the bark off the trees to make that place. Put the bark in the fire and straightened them pieces out and they were just like slabs then. We lived in that for a while. Then he got a house. When we were there some of the Cumera people, those fellas from other tribes, they'd cross over to Kilmore and Murchison and all them places 'cos they knew some whites there, to work, you know? They'd be down there for a week or so and they'd come back, put off at our place and look for a sandy bank. They'd stay all day and all night, then go back to the Cumera

Mission.' Ivy's face softened into a dreamy smile. 'That was when we had our own place we called Madowla.'

'They took the bark to make their canoes as well,' Louie added. 'There's some trees up the lakes with the bark taken off, but I don't remember them doing it. You've seen them, Jean.'

'The canoe trees? My brother told me about the time my father made a canoe,' Jean answered. She had sat quietly listening to the older women. 'Dad always kept it down the river at night for spearing fish. I told my brother that I never saw it and he said Dad used to sink it under the water to preserve the bark.' Jean leaned over to the fire and prodded the burning wood with the poker.

While Mrs Louie Atkinson and Jean Egan were relating the tree-barking events Mrs Ivy Sampson's mind was probing into the past and she continued her story as though there had been no interruption.

'After my mother died my father took me back to Coranderrk, but my brothers and sisters wouldn't leave Cummeroogunga. I was eight years old before he took 'em. Three years later he married another woman. She was a widow and she had a lot of children and I grew there for a long time. Then I used to come back to Cumera, eh Louie?' Turning her face to her friend she called, 'Louie.'

'Yes, you did. Go on about your father.'

'He married Jemima, Bob Wandin's widow. He came from Healesville way but Jemima was born in the Murray district somewhere. We don't know who her mother was, but her father was white. Burns was his name. She was little when her mother died and she was out at the camps. Jemima was very fair. Mr Matthews took her to Coranderrk. You know them prisoners that come out here from England? They were in camps. Worked for settlers.' 'Those convicts were a nuisance amongst our people,' Louie agreed.

'They caused trouble amongst the dark people,' Ivy said and made many references to them during our conversations.

'Jemima was my stepmother, but a good one. She was very kind to me and she treated me like her own, so I was her tenth child. There was Ellen, Robert, Willie, Frank, Jimmy, Joey, Mary, Jessie ad Martha. I grew up with the younger Wandins, Jessie and Martha. The others were grown up.'

'Now Auntie Ivy, you remember all about the Old People. Did you ever hear about my great-grandfather getting drowned?' Louie asked.

'Yes, that was Harry Briggs. He drowned when his wife, Louie, and him lived at Coranderrk. Don't know where it happened.'

'She told me she never married again, but they already had Jack, Maggie, Carrie, Polly and Daisy,' Louie told us. Ivy nodded her head, smiling as Louie continued about the Briggs extended families scattered about Victoria and lower New South Wales.

' 'Cause you know your great-granny Louise was that poor Trucanini's daughter, the one they kept the bones of in Tasmania,' Ivy said, conversationally.

'Yes, we've always been told she was our grandmother's mother. Now,' Louie spoke directly to me, 'where I come from is Maggie Briggs, because she married Leonard Kerr. He grew up on the Goulburn where that white fella, Curr, had some of the country. There's canoe trees out there where his people took the bark to make them. They took it for dishes and other things.'

'That's right,' Ivy replied quickly. It was clear she thought people were more interesting than trees at this stage. 'Old Leonard Kerr from Wyuna way, one of their children was Connie. She married Richard Joyce.'

Louie picked up the theme. 'First there was Thomas Joyce, a white man, and he married full-blood Minnie Podham and they had Richard. He married Connie Kerr and they had me, and my brothers and sisters. Dad was very dark.'

Ivy moved to the edge of her chair and tapped Louie's knee. 'This one here,' she said, and turned to me saying, 'had a sister named Maggie and she had a big family.'

'Oh, sixteen they tell me,' Louie informed us.

At any time it only took one name or question to have Ivy happily recount the family tree concerned.

'Mostly girls' Ivy announced, undisturbed. 'There were about five boys. Maggie was named after her grandmother, and Louie here, was named after her great-grandmother.' She waved her hand at Louie.

'Her mother come from a big family; there was Meena, Connie –' she nodded her head at Louie, '- your poor mother – then poor Lizzie, poor Lennie, poor Archie, poor Rita and Ina.'

'She had a big family alright.'

'Yes, big family alright' Ivy acknowledged.

'And then my own brothers and sisters –' Louie began.

'Lennie, Frankie, poor Ada, poor Maggie, and you.' Ivy finished.

'There was Thelma, too,' Louie reminded her friend. 'She was older than Ada.'

Louie sat for a while, silent. No one spoke. We waited. When she did continue her voice was soft and low, talking more to herself than to us.

'My grandparents, Maggie and Leonard Kerr, must have moved to Cummeroogunga in the big shift from Maloga when George Bellenger took over from Mr Matthews. They must have brought their family there because my mother grew up on the Mission and they lived in one of the houses brought there from Maloga. It's still there now on the Mission. The only one left from Maloga.' Louie sighed and added, 'I was born in that house.'

'That's right,' Ivy announced. 'I know it.' She touched her friend's knee gently. 'Isn't it nice talking about the old days, eh Louie?'

'I always like talking about those times. There were some good times,' Louie replied softly. 'Some real happy times.' Her wistful tone prompted me to leave the two friends to their spoken memories and private thoughts. Jean and I took the opportunity to make a cup of tea for the two elderly, happy ladies.

Chapter Two

Missions with Ivy, Louie and Jean

'It must have been about when you were born at Cumer, Louie, that my father took me to Coranderrk,' Ivy said.

'Probably was, Auntie. My father came from Narrandera. He was twenty-four when he married my mother in Echuca and I was the last of their children to be born. That was in 1908. Dad was a fisherman and we moved from place to place and lived mostly in mia-mias on the river banks. From Narrandera to Wagga back to Narrandera and then over to Darlington Point where the Warangesda Mission was on the Murrumbidgee.'

'The people did some of the buildings and gardens at that Mission. They cleared some of the reserve and farmed it,' Ivy added.

'We were near the Mission for a good time. I didn't get much schooling because we travelled around a lot, and also I spent a lot of time swimming in the rivers. We were living on the river bank near Warangesda when I got appendicitis. Dad was fishing there at the time. It was around about the First World War because I remember the one who carried me up to the Mission. His name was Jimmy Malleebox, an Aboriginal man. He went to the war and was killed.'

'Which hospital did they take you to?' Jean asked.

'It was too late to take me to a hospital because it was twelve miles to Whitton and about forty to Narrandera, so I was operated on in the manager's house. On their dining- room table. After the operation they carried me back on a stretcher to stay the rest of the night with Granny Murray in her cottage. You know, when I had that operation the doctor said the appendicitis was caused by swallowing all the water and sand when I was swimming. The sand just clogged up in there and formed this little ball in the gut.'

Ivy shook her head in wonderment, opened her hands to the fire and murmured, 'You were lucky the doctor came in time. There were a lot of cottages and people there about that time, eh Louie?'

'Yes, a lot of families. My father had a wagonette, so the next day he put me in it on the stretcher and took me to the train at Whitton and I went from there to Narrandera. Later on we lived at Wagga and I went to school at St Mary's. After that we come back this way. My father made all his own fishing nets and his boats. He had about five men fishing for him and at certain times they would travel back up to Darlington Point from Cumera, and fish there.'

Warangesda Mission school teachers's cottage. (Courtesy Gisella Barber, Western Riverina Community Library 1989)

'You lived in that house at Cumera where your mother and grandmother had lived. The one that's still there.'

'That's the one,' Louie said and added almost in a whisper, 'My mother died there.'

'Some of the old People that left Warangesda come to Cumera and others went to Moonacullah Mission,' Ivy said. Louie explained to me, 'That's about twenty miles out of Deniliquin.'

Ivy continued. 'In the very early days of no white people and no convicts about, the tribal people travelled in their own lands. After the white men came it was different, and so were the babies. There were those what you call them about then, those convicts from England, they took the women. One of the Old People told me that when she was born she was not properly dark. The Old Fella, her father the dark one, put her in a stump and left. The mother had no say. Her brother come and got her out of the stump.'

'I've heard that story. It's true,' Louie said.

'When my husband, Berty Sampson, was born, it was back in the early days and he wasn't registered because his family was walking about the country. He was born at Moolpa, at one of those stations down there out of Deniliquin. They were called the Edward River people. Berty's mother was Aggie Gardner and everyone called her Cookaggie. His father was named William Sampson. Old Bill. He was a real dark man. And that old fella was older than Cookaggie was.'

Louie asked, 'Who were their children?'

'Eddie, Nora, Berty, Walter, Syddie, Norman, Theodore and Ellen.That was the Sampson family. They all had big families in those days. The people used to say, 'Old Sampson belonged to the Edward.' There were a lot from the Edward River and they talked the same language. They were first at another place but a man named Dawn wanted that land. He was going to buy it so they got a piece of ground near the Edward and some other creeks and that's where Moonacullah Mission was formed. They built mud huts at first to live in, and that's where the Sampsons lived – and the Days, the Ingrams, the Ross family – oh, a lot of people at Moona. Some come for a while then they'd go off working somewhere on the white fellas stations.'

Ivy and Bery Sampson in Easter 1963. The photo was taken by Alan Burrage, 'Near Cummeragunja on the Murray River. (Courtesy Winifred Burrage)

Moolpa Station between Deniliquin and Moulamein. Dr Pulteney Mein and his brother held thousands of acres and they had plenty of Ivy's 'convict Englishmen' working on the Moolpa property. The tribal camps of the women and girls were constantly raided by white men. Most of the people from Moonacullah Mission went down to Barham, Koondrook and Swanhill.

'The Days were related to the Egans,' Jean gently contributed.

'Oh yes,' Ivy said. 'Old Billy Day was one of the Old People who worked with the whites. Nice old man, and he had a good name, too. I don't know where he came from but he worked during the week out at Colimo Station not far from Moona and he'd come back to the Mission for the weekends. He was married to Maria and they had a good many children. That old man worked on the station riding his horse about 'til the day he died. Their grandchildren and great-grandchildren are about now, some in Echuca I know. Their daughter, Nancy, married an Egan.'

'That was Robert Egan who married Nancy Day.'

'That's right. Then there were the McGees, Taylors, Hamiltons, Edmunds, Ingrams, Robinsons. Old Granny Robinson lived for a long time at Moona and she had a little dog she called Nappy and she was always talkin' to him. Granny died in her sleep in a house on the Mission. Granny's daughter married Galway. The Galways were there and they went down to Barham afterwards. And the Seymours. Old Lily Seymour died in Shepparton.'

In 1883 Johnny Galway wrote from the Cobran Station east of Barham in New South Wales, to the Victorian Board for Protection of Aborigines, requesting two railway passes for two young women living at the station. They were Bella Green and Maggie Edgar. They wished to return to live at Coranderrk. William Goodall, the manager of Coranderrk at that time, believed it was a good idea as they were Victorians and had been residents at Coranderrk. They would also be valuable assistants in the orphanage.

'Lily was a Briggs,' Louie said. 'I thought my mother wasn't dead when I saw her. I've never seen two people more alike.'

'Yes. She was descended from Trucanini of course,' Ivy recalled. 'Lily's mother was Maggie Taylor from Moona, and Maggie married your uncle, Bill Briggs, and they had Lily. She married Billy Seymour, a white man, and they had Syd and Billy. It was one of those boys, Syd or Billly, who come to see me here, and he put a pound in my hand, but I didn't want to take it.'

During the 1950s Bill and Lily's son, Billy, and my husband played in the Edward River Football League. We lived in Barham as did the Galway family. Syd Seymour died in 1985.

'One of Lily's boys made himself known to me the other day,' Louie fitted in.

'I knew their mother right back,' said Ivy. 'We were on Tulla, up from Barham near Wakool, rabbiting – her husband was too – and we'd see each other and have a good old talk. She was nice, I liked her. Even when she shifted to Deniliquin and we was coming from Moona we'd pull up on the river and she'd come down for water and stand there talking.'

'When she shifted to Shepparton she came to visit me in Echuca,' Louie told Ivy. 'I thought my dead mother had come back. The spitting image. She even had a tooth out on the side.' Louie showed us the exact spot.

'Mrs Galway was a McGee,' Ivy went on, her train of thought

never dwindling. 'We used to call her Brooms because she had straight hair the colour of broom,' she said, laughing at the thought as she settled deeper in her armchair. 'Mrs Galway made lovely flowers out of birds' feathers. They were another lot that went to Barham near Koondrook to live.'

Ivy commenced another run-down on the descendants of the Moonacullah Old People. 'Many of them moved to those two townships and to Swanhill and Echuca.'

'The Moona women did make beautiful feather-flowers and they made lovely baskets too, and they'd sell them. Remember?'

'Yes. Made the baskets out of the rushes that grow along the swamps. All that's forgotten now. They don't do it any more,' Ivy murmured regretfully. 'They're easy to make.'

'I did make baskets once but never carried on with it. Do you remember how the Moona people had a different language?' Louie asked.

A group of Coranderrk residents. (Courtesy Jean Baum)

'They talked in their own language and their children learnt it. Very seldom you'd hear any English in those early days.'

'It was different at Cumera. We children didn't learn any. Oh well, we picked up a few words but the Cumera people didn't like going to Moona because they talked in their language and the Cumera ones would think they were talking about them.'

'It was the way they were,' Ivy recollected smilingly. 'They were a funny lot. They didn't like strangers, sometimes Tulla men going around their place.' She turned in her chair. 'Not many of the Moona people came down to Cumera, eh Louie!'

Strangers were people belonging to another tribe. Tulla was in Wamba Wamba country. In a reversed situation the men from Moonacullah would have been the strangers.

'No, not then.'

'My husband, Berty, talked his own language and the strangers that didn't understand him, nicknamed him Frenchy because they reckoned he talked like a Frenchman. I was with him one day in a fishing boat with some others when him and Stanley Day went up the front and was talking together – going at it in their language. All the other people were lookin' at them and lookin' at me.'

'That's why we never liked going up there because they'd all be talking in their own lingo and we didn't know if they were talking about us – or – you know, Auntie.'

Louie finished with a knowing look at Ivy which was captured in the hushed broken sentence. It was obvious the blind woman picked up the mysterious inference but chose not to comment.

'When I lived there after I'd married Berty they still didn't like strangers coming around. They'd talk about them and I could understand what they were saying by then. In the days the Moona men worked on the different stations that belonged to the whites. They'd go off with their swags on their backs to the shearing sheds. Of course there would be other fellas from different tribal places working at the same stations, like the five men from Tulla one day. The Moona men; there was Trotter – that's Jimmy Charles, and Tommy Cameron, oh, a lot of them. They talked about the Tulla men, the strangers. Then they told the Tulla men they couldn't take the Moona boat to cross the river. There was a fisherman coming past in his motor boat and the Tulla men sang out to him and asked him to cross them. They went with him across the Edward.'

Louie supported her friend's account of the distances covered by the people to their employment. 'Everyone had to travel a lot to get to work,' she told me.

'Yes, men and women, they worked on the white stations.' Ivy said. 'I cooked at Colimo Station but that wasn't so far from Moona, but I cooked at other stations, too. For the shearers. One time when the Sampsons were shearing I had nothing for them to have for pudding so I cooked quandongs. Oh, they were lovely. They all had a good feed.'

'We used to get quandongs, too. There's one growing at Moama. They're round and red with a big seed. Louie looked at me and added, 'the kids played marbles with the seeds.'

The quandong tree is now rare in Victoria. The flavour of the fruit is like that of the black guava. The bark of the tree was used by the tribal people for tannning animal skins, and the nuts were made into necklaces.

'A lot of the people had nicknames,' Ivy volunteered, not to be sidetracked by Louie's games of marbles. 'Old Cookaggie called her husband Bang. That meant man. Woman was layook. There was Ettie Edwards, she was Jarves. She married Johnny Charles and he was called Moonyame. Barney Day's nickname was Irish.'

Mrs Atkinson, Mrs Sampson and Mrs Egan discussed the tribal words used by the Old People for English words, and particular areas. They talked about the differences between the Yotti Yotta and surrounding languages. Jean walked over to the fireplace and dropped a log on the fire.

'About twenty years ago my mother-in-law, Nancy Egan, wrote out a lot of the language used at Moonacullah.'

Ivy turned her head sharply towards Jean.

'That fire still burning, Jean?' She had followed Jean's movements and her concern regarding the fire over-ruled the language question.

'Yes, I've just put a log on for you.'

'You put a big one on?'

'Yes, Auntie.'

'Ohhh, Jean.' A decidedly tone of worry was in Ivy's voice. 'Will it be right? I thought it would last you for the night.'

'No. I'm frightened in the night. Might role.'

'I'll fix it up so it won't, Auntie Ivy.'

‘I’ll put it out with water before I go to bed.’

‘Auntie Ivy,’ Louie said. ‘I still never brought those bricks I promised you to put along the front.’ She stood up and took a couple of steps closer to the fireplace. ‘Just a few will keep the fire safe. I’ll get them for you,’ she finished apologetically.

‘When I was little and lived at Coranderrk, I’d see the old men light up their fires,’ Ivy said, recapturing her earlier days. ‘They’d have some wood with a little hole in it and they’d put some bark underneath, then with a little stick taken from a certain tree, and not much smaller than a switch, they’d get the fire going by putting the little stick in the hole and rubbing, and you’d see the smoke coming up. They’d lift the little stick and blow on the bark. Next minute it’d be blazing.’

Ivy smoothed her skirt with her hands. ‘I often wish I had it here when I’ve got no fire going.’

Chapter Three

Moonacullah with Paul Egan

In 1983 Paul Egan was proud of his family and was ready and eager to tell me the stories and events surrounding the lives of his family:

'I've been told that my great-grandfather was an Irishman and he married a dark woman. He came with a lot of other Irish people when they were brought to Portland to work for the white men who had taken up the land. He died young but my Aunt Lucy has a picture of him wearing a long beard. This great-grandfather of mine was a bullock trainer, driving them four at a time.

'My own father, Robert Wallace Egan, was born at the Aboriginal Station at Lake Condah in the Western District of Victoria. He later lived at Framlingham Mission. His brothers were Bill and Jack and his sisters were Lucy, May and Hilda. They were all at the Framlingham Mission and lived there nearly all their lives. They had their cows on Framlingham and never seemed to want for anything, although if they left the Mission sometimes, they got into trouble from the manager.

'Lake Condah, north-east from Portland, commenced in 1867. Just over 2000 acres of land were reserved two years later in the tribal country of the Gournditch-jmara tribe with the southern portion bordering Darlot's Creek. In 1865 the Church of England Mission to the Aborigines operated on some 2,5000 acres of land north-east of Warrnambool reserved beside the Hopkins River, and known as Framlingham. The 1876 records show that Rosa and Mary Egan had young babies, 'but both women were suffering pains.' In 1882 James Egan, with his wife and family, were living at Framlingham. James had asthma and William Goodall, the manager, 'administered a mixture.'

'My grandmother, Maria, was real fair. She married Billy day and they lived at Moonaculla Mission. People know that place there now as Old Marago, out past Pretty Pine. They had my mother Nancy - she was born at the Mission - and Cora, Hilda, Henry, Barney, Stanley, Hubert and Clive. The whole family continued to live at Moona. When my mother married my dad we left the Mission but we used to go back there to visit and for holidays. We'd all go in a horse and cart.

'I was born at Swan Hill in 1940, but the family home was at Barham. We stayed on living in Barham for some time after I was born, but when I was a small child the family was removed for a reason I do not know.'

Framlingham Mission residents. (Courtesy Maisie Clarke)

As late as the 1950s Aboriginal children were not permitted in the Barham swimming pool. The township of Barham on the Murray River in New South Wales was settled by Edward Green in 1843. He gave the area his wife's maiden name, Barham. The Murray separates Barham from Victorian Koondrook. The Baraparapa tribal word, *koondrook,* means moon.

'At Moona I remember Mum having long talks with an old Aboriginal lady named Lil Seymour. She was a great old lady and I was often at her place with Mum. Old Lil kept sugar and other things in jars with lids on and I used to like looking to see what was in them. One day Old Lil caught me lifting the lid off on one of them. She cracked me on my hand, pushed the lid down and said, "there's no sugar in there," and sent me off.

'There was another old lady there named Cookaggie. All her children were dead, and every night they reckon that she cried for them. She liked me and when we went there to visit I'd do odd jobs for her, like cutting her wood and bringing it in for her. I didn't think it was a lot of work but she'd give me a big handful of money when I'd finish and I thought I was overpaid. I suppose she wanted to give me a bit of money, but not let me think I could get it just for nothing.

'There was a Church, a missionary house, a school and at least forty houses at Moona. A windmill on the river pumped the water for the Mission. There was a manager on the station, and one time his small son was running up the hill carrying a bottle and he fell, tripped on a stone. He cut his jugular vein and died. The school closed up after that, and a minister from Deniliquin came out for services for the people.

'The men made mud bricks for some of the farm houses and when the little jobs run out they reckoned the clay was so good there that they made more bricks to sell outside the Mission. The comradeship between the people was strong at Moona. The men were well dressed. Every year they sent away to Sydney for black suits. Hats and white shirts, too. And they wore bow ties.

'Mum's brother, Uncle Stan, told us lots of stories when we were little kids. One I remember was about when the missionaries were there, and things were tough for them and the people. There was a farmer near Moona once, named Duffy, and he would sometimes drop off a sheep at the Mission for the people.

'One day Uncle Barney was near the Mission House and he heard the missionary saying the prayers at the table. He saw the family through the window, sitting there at the table for their meal and the missionary was praying to God for bread. He told his family that if they had faith in their prayers they would get bread. Uncle Barney went off and got hold of some freshly made damper, came back to the missionary's window and threw it in onto the table. Uncle Stan said that Uncle Barney got the missionary's prayer answered for him.

'I've heard the men at Moona talk about the turtles and

how they would eat them. I saw a bloke cook one once, and I had some of it. Didn't like it too much. Uncle Stan told us how they used to dive in the river for the crayfish. They ate a lot of that. Yellowbelly, too. The Edward River is at Moona and the Aborigines were able to get plenty of fish. My cousin, Wesso day, was a great fisherman. Never told anyone where he went. Just like it was a gold mine. That was when he fished the Edward at Moona.

'Wesso knows some of the old language but we couldn't understand it. We never learned it. Mum and Uncle Stan would sit for hours talking in their language but we never tried and Mum never made us. During the 196s Professor Hercus and his wife came to see my mother and they got the language from her. It's in a book now.

This language material is available at the Australian Institute of Aboriginal Studies, Canberra.

'The men living on the Mission got work outside when they could. It was mainly shearing and station work on the big places like Boolpool. They could be away from their homes at Moonacullah for perhaps three months at a time. When they got back they always had plenty to talk about. They'd tell each other what went on at the different stations; who they met; what they did. They'd tell those yarns over and over again.

'In those days the Old People were very frightened of ghosts. Spirits. Some even today. Maybe it is the fear that their parents put into them. You know, they talked about the *goon*. To us, too, when we were kids. It was a dog they saw about the place at night, mostly on moonlight nights. They saw it. Uncle Stan saw it. He said it was a big dog. The people used to stop the kids from going outside by telling them, "*goon* dog is there looking through the window," and the kids behaved themselves.

'Probably this fear of unknown things put an idea into Uncle Willie Day's head. He was a drover. He was a poet, too. He wrote his poems. Anyway, he thought he would frighten all the others at the Mission. There used to be a lot of wild South Australian Aborigines come past Moona when he was a boy. Wild ones they were. Nearly every night the people could see them coming, carrying their spears and no clothes on except a sort of loin covering. They'd just pass by going somewhere.

'One night Uncle Willie wrote a note, pretending it was from the wild ones, and he left it on the tap for the Mission people to find. In the note he made out he was a wild Aboriginal and that he and the others were waiting in the bush to attack the people. That letter caused a lot of trouble at Moonacullah. Everyone was scared and they all talked about the note to each other. At last they decided to have a meeting in the hall about it. All the people went and so did the missionary and the teachers.

'One of the Moona blokes said they were all going to be slaughtered by these wild Aborigines, 'and you know what slaughter is' he told them. They wanted to get the police. Then one of the teachers woke up. Common sense would have told the people that the wild Aborigines couldn't write, but they were too scared to think of that at the time. The teacher kept asking who wrote the note until he finally found out that it was Uncle Willie.

'There's a place called Willow Bend, down from Moonacullah, were no-one will camp. [At this point Paul's wife says it's creepy and shudders]. There were times when Uncle Stan would be out fishing in his canoe and he'd drift near Willow Bend. Sometimes he could hear a bloke in a boat singing, 'Does your mother come from England or from Ireland' and he could even hear chains rattling on the boat. There never was anyone there though, so it could have been the spirit of one of the early squatters. Whenever Uncle Stan heard this singing he'd just go away from the place. He thought he wasn't supposed to be there, and he'd move on somewhere else. Those sort of things could happen in the bush, too.

'On night at the Mission, one old bloke wanted to get a drink for one of his kids who was crying. He had to go outside the house for the water because the taps were out there. They used to fill kero buckets with water. When his wife heard him go she was too frightened to stay inside without him and, unknown to him, she quietly followed him out the door to the kero bucket. The old bloke got such a fright when he heard a noise behind him that when he saw it was his wife he really went crook at her.

'There's a story told about two old blokes who went to pinch some oranges at Barham – there were a lot of oranges grown there. Now neither of these fellas knew that the other was anywhere around because they got into the orange grove from different directions. It was just on dark before they reached it, and each man heard the noises coming from the opposite side. They didn't stop to see who was there, or to speak. They just took off with fright. Neither of them thought it was just another man on the other side of the orange tree, and they didn't wait to find out either.

'When I was at Balranald not long ago an Aboriginal fella named Tom Kelly told me about the blackfella who was clever in the days when there were no cars. This clever man was at Balranald and he saw four or five Aborigines come in from Cummeroogunga. He went to them and told them he knew where they were camping and which house they were in; where they were going to work – and he was right. Then he said to one of them, 'You made the fire.' The Cumer man said, 'Yes, I did.' This clever old fella went on to tell them who was sleeping where, and all sorts of things. He was right every time.

'The Cumera men asked him how he knew all these things and he said, 'See those white mice near that hole?' They said yes they did. 'I was one of them and I saw everything.' These Cummeroogunga men just looked at him, frightened of him, because they knew then that he was a medicine man.

'Now my theory is that the old blackfella had tremendous powers of observation. He noticed things. He had probably seen these men before and knew how they camped, and where, and who they usually saw when they went to Balranald, and where they worked. Those clever fellas were very smart. They used their skills to make the people frightened. One thing about them. They always got a good night's sleep. They had no-one to be frightened of, but the other people did. They were always scared of them.

'There was a power the people had of connecting up with each other when they were miles apart. Uncle Stan was a great bushman, and he told me once that when he was camping in the bush he heard his brother coming along the track to his camp.

He heard him lean his bike against the wire fence. When he turned to speak to him he wasn't there. Uncle Stan was worried about his brother for a while after that. He thought there could be something wrong with him, but he was alright.

'I believed that story. Uncle Stan had no need to lie about it to me. He just sat there telling me that yarn while he smoked his pipe at the bush campfire.

'Christmas times were great on the Mission. Underneath the two big cork trees there, six or seven tables were set up and all the people would sit together with the food they brought, including puddings with threepenny pieces in them. We call the trees 'cork' because they have a corky sort of a trunk, but I think they're elm trees.

'There were good times at Moona, and sad. One of the worst times for the people was when the police come and took the little kids away and put them in places hundreds of miles away in New South Wales and Queensland where they were supposed to be taught farming and housekeeping. The police were sent in by the Government to take the kids from the parents. They were dressed up with revolvers, too, and they had handcuffs. A lot of policemen resigned because of this. They said it was a terrible thing to have to do.

'My Dad was always a great worker. I can't remember him ever being sick although I suppose there must have been times, but he had ten kids to feed and keep clothed so he had to keep on the go.

'We came to live in Echuca in an old house where this one is built. Right here. Dad eventually owned this block and that house that was on it.

'He did pick and shovel work for a bloke who lived not far away from here. His name was Mullane, a real nice, quiet sort of a bloke. Then he got onto the Railways and stayed there until he retired when he was sixty-five. He didn't stop work even then. He went out and worked for the saw mills until he got too old. They thought it was too dangerous for him. When he died it was a big funeral. Al the shops closed their doors while the cars went by. He was a good father to us. Everything he did, he did in moderation.

Never smoked heavy or never drank to excess.

'Mum died in 1965 and Uncle Stan is dead, too. There is only Aunt Cora left in Swan Hill and an uncle in Deniliquin.

'My brother, Bob, was a great footballer and he coached teams, too. There was another Egan who played for Carlton in the 1930s. He'd have been one of our crowd.

'My sister was marred to Fred Walker, son of Old Fred Walker from Barmah. They had ten kids and they lived at Moonacullah Mission. But he was a Cumera man and people from different tribes don't get on well, especially on a Mission, staying here. They moved off and took their family to Dandenong. Others moved from the Mission too, when they were offered homes in Deniliquin.

'A strange thing happened to me once, in this house, when I was sitting talking with my cousin in the front room. Now, before this house was built, we lived in the old one, and there was a big piece of concrete block around it. This night when I was with my cousin we heard a man walking along that concrete, but it wasn't there anymore. It was under the earth! He walked along the concrete and we could hear his steps clearly. We could even hear the leather squeaking in his boots, and you don't hear that anymore in boots. We heard it as it came closer, then the steps passed the room and we heard them go round the house. I looked at my cousin and he was just sitting staring, listening. After a while we got up and went outside and looked around the house. No one there.

Fred Walker in his home in 1983.

'A long time ago my Grandmother told us the story of two women and their children. This was a story to learn something from.

'A woman in the tribe had only one child and she could not have any more. Another woman had sixteen children. The first woman killed an animal, then showed the remains to the other woman. 'Look' she said. 'I have killed one of my children. You have sixteen. That is too many. You should kill one like I have done.' And the woman killed one of her babies. After a few days the first woman killed another animal, made it look like a child, and went to the other woman again. 'Look, I have killed another one. You do the same.' The woman did that, too. And so it went on until the first woman had got the second woman to kill all her children. She had none left. The first woman still had her child.

'The moral of that story is that you should never let people talk you out of what you believe to be right, or to do what other people want you to do, just to be like them.

'Be happy with what you have yourself '.

Chapter Four

Lover's Lane

'Cumera,' Ivy breathed. 'It was beautiful. Just over there,' she explained to me, pointing her finger to the river, seeing beyond it quite vividly in her mind. 'Like a town. A beautiful Mission in our young days.'

While Ivy was speaking Louie's head was fixed in a continuous nod, her cheeks flushed and her blue eyes shining.

'The streets were all gravelled,' Ivy said, raising her arms and holding them wide apart, ' and there were three shops. Huey Anderson and Sons. He had that on a board outside his shop.'

In 1885 Huey visited Nathalia with Thomas Shadrach James to address a Church congregation, and again to Picola with Paddy Swift for a Service. He and his family were amongst those taken from Maloga to Cumeroogunga where conditions caused unhappiness. In 1892 he returned to Daniel Matthews at Maloga, destitute, taking with him his wife and their five children. Eventually the family lived at Cumergunga where he later had the shop.

'Huey married Ellen, a relation of Louie's mother-in-law. She was from up the coast way, and they had ten children. They sold anything; fruit, lollies, drinks, and they had ice cream, too. Then there was Henry and Maggie Nelson's shop. I know she used to make the ice cream herself because us kids would go and buy it. She made it the hard way, with the churn. The other shop belonged to Les Firebrace and his family. Cumera was just like a village. After my father took me to live at Coranderrk I used to still come back here, eh Louie? Louie knows.'

'Yes. Go on, Auntie,' Louie encouraged.

'There was the big Government store and the meat shop. That store opened every morning at 9 o'clock and you could even buy a pair of dungarees, what they called them in those days.

Buy anything. On Friday morning they'd ring the bell to let the people know they were ready to give out a few rations. Remember the meat shop, Lou?' A murmur from her friend was enough. 'Fresh chops, or whatever. Then when the milk bell rang they'd go up with their jugs to get it.'

'Billycans, too.'

'Poor old Andy Alton, your Uncle Andy, Lou.'

'That's right. He married my Auntie, Carrie Briggs.'

'He'd go for his milk. He was blind and he'd go along hitting the fence with his walking stick till he got to the shop for the milk.'

'Stone blind, but he could go anywhere. Grill his chops, do anything,' Louie answered and a laugh quickly followed. 'Aunt Carrie used to like having a bit of lace showing from her petticoat.' Louie touched Ivy's hand. 'I wish you could see, Auntie Ivy. I'd like you to take me over there to the Mission to see something.'

Ivy Sampson, capturing the past.

'I know what you're looking for,' Ivy said, turning her eyes to me. 'She's looking for Lovers' Lane, what we called it.' She laughed with Louie.

'She knows,' Louie said, raising her eyebrows at Ivy. 'I've been over there and can't find it.'

'It was at the back of the old Mission. The streets are different now. We couldn't find Lovers' Lane,' Ivy told Louie, sorrowfully. 'The streets were called Cooper, George and Chandler, but they're gone and there's different ones. They've put houses in other places, too. It's all changed now.'

'They've mucked us up now, Auntie Iyy. Well, how far was Lovers' Lane from the school that's there now?'

'Oh, well,' Ivy began, and between them the women established the whereabouts of the disappeared Lovers' Lane.

After a well-deserved cup of tea and a few minutes rest Ivy pursued her reliable memories.

'There was another blind one at Cumera when I was little, called Johnny Swift. His mother had a shop at Moama and my mother was staying with her when she was sick and when she had to go into hospital I was allowed to live with them for a while. Johnny had a brother, Eddie, but it was Johnny and me that played up on the Echuca-Moama Bridge. We'd be up there when the train would come along. I'd get out of the way. I'd run off. But do you know what Johnny would do? He'd get on the side and sit on his bag. The bridge would be shakin' as the train was going over. Johnny wouldn't run away. Wonder he never used to fall. After the train was gone past I'd go back and I'd look. He'd be there.'

'Blind,' Louie added.

'Yes, and hangin' on there like somethin' on the side of the bridge. I'd be frightened but he'd stay. He went around the Mission with a bike wheel without spokes, rolling it, waving his stick in front of his eyes. Everyone loved Johnny at Cumera. When he was older he could pump the water, drive the engine, do anything. He could recognize people from their voices when they'd been away for five or six years from the Mission.'

'After his first wife died he married my Aunt Dinah.'

'Yes. There was Jenny Swift in these parts once. We don't know much about her, do you Lou? Johnny and Eddie went to the war you know.'

Jenny was one of the young women taken to Maloga from Queensland. Paddy belonged to the Bangerang, his tribal area was between the King and Ovens rivers. They met at Maloga, where they were married, and went to England on Mission work. They returned to live at Warangesda. Jenny died in 1893.

'There were about fifty houses along the streets one time,' Louie said to me. 'The people that lived at Cumera. Granny lived on one of the street corners in the same street Sophy lived. There was the little place where Sir Doug was born, and next door was where poor Auntie Ellie Campbell died. The Coopers, Clements, Barbers. So many.'

'We had an old Eddison gramophone and we'd play records and the boys and girls would listen to them, then they'd dance in the streets.'

Louie agreed wholeheartedly, both going into peals of laughter. 'I wouldn't mind having one of those antique gramophones now.'

f

'Seems the Briggs families all loved dancing and music,' Louie answered.

In 1879 Jack Briggs, with his wife, two daughters and a son, were at the Ebenezer Mission in the Wimmera District of Victoria, Reverend Kramer, the manager, complained bitterly that the Briggs children danced in the bush when they thought he was not about. He wanted the family removed apart from one of the girls who was ill. He was concerned also that the large number of Briggs would have a strong influence on other Aborigines regarding disobedience of regulations.

'You remember poor old Marky – that's her nickname, she was Margaret – how she used to sing? She smoked a stumpy pipe, too. One of those without the stem. I often wondered why they did that.'

'Granny Briggs smoked a stumpy pipe,' Ivy said.

'I never knew that,' Louie said in surprised. 'Mum never did and I never did either.'

'Yes,' said Ivy, untroubled about her friend's shock to learn Granny was a stumpy-pipe-smoker. 'They'd sing down at Marky's and you'd hear them singing hymns in the night. The Anderson boys would be there singing, too.'

'You'd hear it all over the town.'

'Other times all the young girls and fellas sang at night in my niece's house that was up near the manager's house. They'd go outside singing away and keep the manager awake. He didn't like it.'

'No, he was just on the other side.' That memory amused both the ladies.

Louie and Ivy talked to each other, recalling the names and marriages of the singers, where they lived and worked. They spoke of one of the older Cumera men who left the Mission after his wife died.

'He was sixty when he went to the Western District to get married again. His childhood sweetheart,' Ivy laughed delightedly and Louie joined in, needing no encouragement at all.

'That's like Lovers' Lane,' she murmured in a dreamy voice. 'That's got to crop up all the time. We're not going to tell any stories about that. Better let it be,' she said with some reluctance.

'Oh, it's a closed book,' Ivy assured her, but her eyes seemed to dance and sparkle in the fireglow, and she could see enough of the delights of Lovers' Lane to send her into great chortles of laughter with her friend.

'There were peppercorn trees all over the Mission,' Louie said at last.

'You're starting again, Louie,' Ivy chided. 'You know, for years we could tell where Lovers' Lane was by where those trees were growing.'

'Yes, and it was my own nephew that cut them down,' Louie groaned.

'If I'd known in time I'd have sent word to him not to take our trees down. He wouldn't have done it then,' Ivy told Louise confidently.

'Big pepper trees,' Louie lamented. 'Lovely shade in the summer.' She brightened. 'They were alright to get under at night, too. I can say that much,' she finished with relish, her eyes twinkling. Louie's tone of voice was distinctly teasing.

Lovers' Lane was not lost to them at all.

Chapter Five

The Facts of the Legends

'Our men had fish-traps in the rivers, you know. They learned that from their fathers,' Louie began. 'Corse these days you have to know where they were to see any sign of them. In the summer there's always a lot of white families along the river, especially where there's a bit of sand.'

'I know there were shells stuck in the banks of the river where, a long time ago, the Old People had feeds of crays and yabbies,' Ivy answered.

'Still there in places, Auntie. When our families swim at Barmah they knew where not to go. Anyway, Aboriginal people around here know.'

'You mean – the Bunyip?'

'Uh-hah.'

There was deafening silence! Even the fire ceased crackling! This was not a subject to be treated with any light-hearted comments. Jean Egan had come with us again to see Ivy but she was not about to further the opening made by Mrs Atkinson. Nor add to Mrs Sampson's. Her gaze was fixed, looking into the leaping flames of the open fire.

After a lengthy time I asked quietly about the Moira tribal people.

'The Dark People?' Ivy asked. 'There was Old Cocky, the old black one. He went up there near the Bunyip Hole.'

After proffering this information Ivy sat still. Very still. She waited. Louie did not speak or move. Jean kept her eyes on the fire. Without moving her head Ivy spoke to me.

'The Bunyip Hole is where the caravan park is near the Barmah Bridge.'

'Old Cocky might have went down in that Bunyip Hole,' Louie uttered in a low voice.

'His boat was found floatin' on the other side and his dog sitting on the bank. Never found his body. His dog died there waiting for him.'

Louie took a deep breath, and asked bravely, 'You know any stories about the Bunyip? Old People ever tell you, Auntie Ivy?'

'Oh, they reckoned he was there all right.' She raised her eyes to the ceiling and placed her hands on the arms of the chair. Leaning slightly towards me without changing the direction of her eyes, she murmured with conviction, 'He's still there.'

'Old Granny Briggs reckoned the Bunyip was living in the river,' Louie's hushed voice reached me.

Coranderrk Men. (Courtesy Jean Cross)

'Up in Narrandera it's the same,' Jean told us. 'We've got one in a big hole where we used to go fishing. We saw it once.' The two older women nodded their heads slowly.

'One night the girls were down there on the river having a party,' Ivy said. 'While they were there up come all the boughs and things out of the water, and they were off.'

'That was the Bunyip stirring it all up,' Louie explained. 'There's been people, Aboriginal and white, who have drowned in this part of the Murray. The stories were they were murdered or committed suicide or just drowned by accident. But I don't know.'

'A long time ago one of those that drowned was a fella called

Roger. He went there to see some boxing fellas he knew. Got drowned on this side where the steep bank is and they couldn't find his body so they had to get the steamer to come down. His body had been washed into the cave but it came up in the end. He was a white fella and he's buried in the Barmah cemetery. Our people talked about the Bunyip.'

'Never talk about it now,' Louie muttered.

'Frank, your poor husband, seen him, didn't he.'

'Yeah. Freddie Walker was with him in the boat and this thing was behind them. Freddie got that much of a fright he was spittin' blood.'

'Yeah,' Ivy nodded.

'One time on the Mission, Frank and I were standing on the top of the bank near the tanks where they pump the water up. Well, this big black thing was moving around in the river but we couldn't see what it was. Whether it was a big black fish or - but it was a big thing. I reckon it was that Bunyip, or,' she added hopefully, 'a big black fish.'

'You think it's not true, eh?' Jean asked, listening intently.

'Well, Frank and I looked. We heard something heavy being thrown in the water. It sounded like -' but Louie could not say anything more.

'It's true all right,' Jean said. 'The Bunyip seems to be all over. I remember on the hill there when all the boys were down on the river and they seen this thing coming out of the water. This slimy grass thing, weeds and all on it.'

'Yes?' Both the women chorused.

'Those boys ran back to my father,' she concluded.

'There's Bunyip at Moonacullah,' Ivy said. 'Young ones, too.'

'When my brother, Frank, was burning charcoal there used to be something come,' Louie told us. 'You'd see it. Just the head part swimming along. We were told to keep our horses away because there was this funny smell, and they reckoned it made the horses play up. I never came in contact with him when I used to swim so much in the river. We'd swim backwards and forwards across the river and I never saw him once then.'

'I don't know if you believe in *bekkers*,' Ivy said, looking straight at Louie as, at the same time, tucking a wisp of escaped hair back behind her ear. Louie did not speak, but her widened eyes betrayed the answer.

'Louie's grandfather on her mother's side was Old Leonard Kerr from Ulupna way. He married Maggie Briggs, remember? Now, Leonard was a Goulburn Tribe man and when they moved onto the Mission those people liked to go back sometimes to their own places. Him and Old Billy Anderson, they'd go off for a few days. Poor Old Billy used to say, 'We're the last of the Goulburn Tribe.' Oh, there was Old George Charles and Billy, and Martin Logan, Samson Barber, a lot of them come from the Goulburn.'

In 1880 George Charles was 23 and Samson Barber 28. Both men were residents of Maloga with permission to work outside the Mission.

'Now, one time when Old George Charles went over to Wyuna two of those *bekkers* come and chased him. He got into a hollow log down on the Deep Creek and they were runnin' around the log trying to get him, talkin' in their own lingo. Anyway they got sick of it and went off. Old George got out of the log and he walked across the river, you could walk across at that place then.' Ivy explained the crossing to me. 'One time when two fellas tried to get across in the junction of Deep Creek it was too deep and they drowned. That's the old yarns they told us.'

'My father told me the *bekkers* were little hairy men,' Louie admitted.

'Yes,' said Ivy. 'There's hairy men up in the mountain way. I've never heard of any of them down here, but there's still some in the caves up there. Down Moona way they call the hairy men nutha. Mad on babies they were those bekkers and nuthas. They'd take the little ones away.'

The front door opened and Frank Atkinson, Louie's son, walked into the room. He had been in time to hear Ivy's last remark.

'Old Grandfather Bull told me they used to run away in the thistles to get away from the *bekkers* and he came from South Australia,' Frank said.

‘They were at Coranderrk, too,’ Ivy told him.

‘They ran along on all fours, and they would stand up and run,’ Louie told Frank.

‘At Coranderrk in those days the men went pheasant shooting up in the mountains,’ Ivy resumed. ‘To climb back down the mountain with their catch they’d fasten the dead pheasant onto their backs. By the time they got down on the flat they wouldn’t have one left on their backs. The bekkers took them and they wouldn’t feel those hairy men doing it. The Coranderrk men reckoned the bekkers sat up there in their caves in the mountains.’

‘What about that child that disappeared,’ Louie prompted.

‘You remember about that boy that was lost at Marysville, Lou? They found the tracks and that was all. The Aboriginal men tracked the boy to the creek bed and they said the Hairy Men had hid him because some of them found one of their caves with papers and things in it.’

A silence followed, much longer than usual. There was a feeling of tension and fearful emotion, as though the incomprehensible things spoken of should not have been discussed; a feeling of regret they had been. Suddenly Jean moved her chair and picked up a length of stick and prodded the log on the fire. Immediately, Ivy felt for the long poke, clasped it firmly in her hand and leaned over to push and shove the embers until tiny flames started to shoot through the wood. Jean knocked the flame out which had caught on the end of her stick. She tapped it on the bricks.

‘Auntie Ivy, you know about Black Doctors.’ Jean sounded as though she did not want to mention them but felt she must do so.

‘Black Doctors.’ Ivy took her time to return the poker to its usual place.

‘Yes.’

‘There was one of them I met,’ Ivy answered slowly, almost unwillingly. There was no sound in the room. At last she spoke, very quietly. ‘I met him at Freddie Walker’s home a long time ago.’

Louie grabbed a moment to break the subject by turning to

me. 'That's Freddie that lives at Moama now, near Cumera. He's Old Sarah Walker's grandson.'

'We called her Mallock,' was Ivy's contribution, her voice much lighter. 'She wore a scarf around her head all the time, or a rag, or whatever she had, no scarves much in them days. Mallock Walker was married to the first Freddie Walker in Mr Matthews' days at Maloga. One of her children was Herbie. The Walkers were some of the first at Maloga Mission. When that little Herbie grew up he married Florrie Hamilton.'

'It was at Florrie's and Herb's place you met that doctor?' Louie suggested.

'That Black Doctor come from – he came as a stranger to us from right up in New South Wales.' Ivy sat without moving. 'Jean? He belonged in your family.'

'Loolbung,' Jean replied, her voice low and without expression.

'Loolbung!' Louie's high pitched exclamation was followed with, 'We were frightened of him.'

'He came to Florrie's with another old fella when I was there one day,' Ivy said, speaking calmly. 'Florrie was his niece, his sister Annie's daughter. Florrie used to give me a shilling to stay at her place when she had to go working at midwifering. She wasn't there when these two came and I was frightened, and I put a paper in front of my face. He was so clever that he took it out of my hand and I didn't know he took it, and I off anyway. He was a doctor alright. He lived at Cumera later on.'

'Yes, he did,' Frank said joining the conversation. 'Old Loolbung blew the horn, an old cow horn, to call us little kids up when he wanted to tell us the stories.'

'A long time ago Loolbung lived at Griffith,' Jean told Frank. 'He lived in a bark hut leaning against a tree. My grandmother used to warn us about going near it.'

'Remember Old Dick Holmes,' Louie said, as though she had been pondering about him for a while before she mentioned him to Ivy.

'Um.'

'You know what went on with him. He was another doctor.'

'Um.' Ivy was not to be drawn yet.

'He wanted my Aunt Meena,' Louie carried on, failing to coax her friend in revealing any stories. Unruffled by Ivy's lack, or fear of, co-operation in this story, she bounced ahead. 'He was after her. Ah, but someone else wanted her. Auntie Ivy's brother, Peter, was sweet on her,' Louie finished triumphantly.

That was too much for Ivy, and the closed pages of the past opened once more.

'Old Dick Holmes wanted Meena for himself, and so did my brother, Peter. Meena liked Peter, and not Dick. Jimmy Charles was the cowboy then at Cumera, had to go out in the paddocks for the cows. A few times on his way he saw Dick going out to the horse paddock and sometimes saw him up in a tree. Anyhow, after a while Peter and Meena both got sick. They got worse. One day Jimmy Charles told Peter he saw Dick Holmes up this tree in the horse paddock every day and they thought it was strange. Meena and Peter were almost dying. Then this day when Jimmy had to go for the cows he saw – he saw this one go up the tree and he watched him. He put something in a tin and pulled something out.'

'Jimmy went back and told Peter.' Louie could not resist helping the story along.

'He did,' said Ivy. 'They went back to the tree together. They found this thing was knockin' in a tin up in the tree. They got it down and threw it in the river. Jimmy and Meena both got better after that, but this doctor, he was going to shoot poor Jimmy.'

Louie was hesitant in finishing the account, 'What the doctors do is, they get your hair and put a bone with it and something, I don't know,' she said, shaking her head. 'I don't want to know either but that's what he had at the horse paddock, just there before you come to the gate that leads in now at Cumera.'

'Ah, poor Peter and poor Meena,' Ivy said, relieved that the story was finished.

'Pretty powerful aren't they,' Jean said.

'I don't like them. I wouldn't live with those sort of people,' Louie confided. 'Too scared.'

It had become overcast outside and the room had darkened. No-one had noticed when Frank had left the gathering. Jean switched the light on. Ivy heard the click.

'The darkness doesn't bother me now,' she said, and laughed.

Chapter Six

The Ways of the Old People

'My father ate the mussels here in the early days,' Ivy told us brightly, launching off into her memoirs. 'They'd put them in the fires and burn them and cook 'em. I never ate them but I did witchetty grubs.'

'They're lovely,' Louie said.

'I'd eat 'em again too,' Ivy drooled. 'My brother Dick, he'd climb up the tree to get them while I waited at the bottom with a billycan.'

'I've had them,' Jean added.

'I'd follow my father round when he was ring-barking and we'd find a lot. He'd cook them in the ashes of the fire,' Louie said. 'They taste like peanut butter.' She touched Ivy's arm. 'Did you ever go out the hills to dig yams?'

Ivy nodded. 'Never hear of them now. They died out with the Old People I suppose. When they all went, the yams must have went too.'

'Anyhow, another thing they ate was molasses. They ate it when they were at Maloga, too. Grandfather Kerr said they had it for the farm machinery to put on the big belts and the strippers, to stop them from slipping around you see. He reckoned they fetched a lot of that stuff home to use on their bread.'

'We had a thing growing here we used to call *buccabund* didn't we, Louie. We'd get it by the armful and we'd all sit down and eat it.'

'We'd take some salt with us and we'd pick *buccabund* in the crop paddocks.'

'It's got a yellow flower on it, but we didn't eat the flowers. We peeled the stems with a knife,'

'put some salt on,'

'and eat them Gee, they were nice.' Ivy concluded.

'You remember Old Granny Morgan, Auntie.'

'Yuppi, we called her.'

Louise Atkinson's medicinal flowers.

'Yes. She'd take us out the bush. She would just round up any kids that would go with.' Louie laughed, and nudged Ivy. 'No wonder we never had any education. Yuppi would take us up to the hill where the pine-trees grow to do some rabbiting. She'd have a roll of wire and a tomahawk and a bag with a bit of damper and salt in it. She knew which log a rabbit was in, and she'd get the wire, put it in and twitch it about, and pull him out. Then she'd kill it and skin it. Old Granny Morgan would make a fire then and cook the rabbit on the coals for us.'

'Go huntin' barefooted. I used to go with her fishing,' Ivy said.

'Barefooted. Yes, we were.'

'She was a real dark old lady and everyone like her. She was pretty nice.'

'Everybody like her,' Louie agreed.

'She was Old Alf Morgan's wife. This Alf was Bagot's cousin, not the brother.'

'Bagot was one of the first little kids at Maloga.'

'This Old Alf, he went away for a while as a sort of a Black Policeman and when he come back to Cumera he'd married Yuppi.'

'What about Granny Wentworth, she was one of the women

that went fishing,'

'Her real name was Granny Benton, wasn't it, Lou. We all called her the other because she had come from Wentworth in the boat, the steamer. She had a sort of a beard.' Ivy moved her hands around the lower part of her face. 'We'd see her down on the river fishing.'

'No boots.'

'No, and she'd tie fishing lines on each of her big toes and throw the lines in the river, and if the fish got caught they'd be pullin' on her toes.'

'She'd have lines here and lines down there, and holding one in her hands as well,' Louie continued. 'She wasn't going to miss any fish. If we said we were going to have blackfish or bream for tea, we'd know where to just go and sit down, and catch them because Granny Wentworth knew.'

'There were ones that used nets, remember?' Ivy lifted her head. 'What about Old Annabella and Old Ned. They were a real old couple when they caught that cod, weren't they Louie? It was at the First and Second Creeks where they had their nets in, and this big fish – he was 100 lbs – was caught in the net. This old couple couldn't put him in the boat. Anyway, Old Ned held the net and Annabella sailed for the land and they got their cod in.'

'They were really old when they got that one,' Louie said. There was another old lady about in those days. Barmah Maggie. She was a full-blood.'

'She used to say, 'I'm Barmah the Maggie.' She was from the Moira tribe. She had a little hut down near the punt and she'd go there with her little billy of beer. Old W.T. had the punt and she looked after the Maloney kids.'

W.T. Maloney. The punt which was owned by Maloney was replaced in 1929 by one which was towed upstream by steamer from Euston to Barmah and was operated by the Department of Main Roads. It was last used as a ferry on the 19 March, 1966, prior to the opening of the new bridge. This old punt now lies in the undergrowth on the bank of the Murray near the bridge and is surrounded by a wire fence with a padlocked gate.

'Barmah Maggie and her little drinks of beer' Louie

murmured. 'I wonder is that mulberry tree still there around the back of the pub. We'd come up from the Mission and raid the mulberries. We knew when the fruit was there.'

'I don't know if it's still growing.' Ivy told Louie. 'Never hear of it now. They might have cut it down. Then you must have been going there for the fruit when Old Barmah Maggie was living in her hut. She died a long time ago, when Old Cumera was there. I worked for the Maloney family later on.'

Louie meditated for a while about the beer and berries before she dealt with another area of their culture.

'The Old People were good with their medicines. They told us about them. We still use Old Man Weed for sicknesses,' Louie assured me. 'You find it growing along the river bank. There's no flower on it.'

'It looks like big a bush of weed and it grows a little thing on it like a pimple.'

'And it looks like pepper if you undo it.'

'You wash the lot and boil it up, then strain it and bottle the liquid.' Ivy showed her enthusiasm for this subject by rubbing and rolling the palms of her hands. 'There's none of the bush about now – no flood – but if you go up where the river is narrower and cross the bridge, that's where there's a lot growing. Our people come to get it, and they send it to their relations as well. One poor woman lately, only had a year to live and her brother come out here and got some for her. She lived two years.'

'You know, Auntie, I was up at the doctor's every week for tablets, so I thought I'd try Old Man Weed again, and I'm real good now. I've got it in a bottle at home. Take it three times a day if I want to.'

Ivy moved her head, approvingly. 'That's good.'

'The marshmallow plant is another one the old women knew about and used it for all sorts of things. I have, too. Once when my son had a badly swollen leg we used it on him and that got all the swelling down. Marshmallow still grows in the paddocks. So do puff balls. We used them for powder for the babies. The adults used it, too. There was no talcum powder then and the women went out and collected the puff balls and we'd break the ball and it was powdery and brown inside. We used that, as talcum powder is used today.'

Louie patted her hair, and sat back in her chair looking contentedly satisfied she had given me some important information about their early days.

'We learned all these things when we were children, and then young women, because the old women were still doing them, weren't they Louie?'

Chapter Seven

The Scourges of Cumera

'There was T.B. amongst the Aboriginal people all over the place as well as at Cumera,' Louie said.

'Sometimes when they were sent from the Mission to another, the T.B. went with them. There was someone who came to visit one of the families at Cumera and stayed in their house and the manager discovered she had T.B. At that time Aunt Meena, Mum's sister, worked for the manager, housekeeping and that sort of thing. This woman – they must have had her in the tent for fresh air – had to have help and Auntie was doing for her. She caught the T.B and it just spread through the family, and all the girls except Mum died from it.'

'Your aunties, Meena, Esssie, Rita and Ina died, and so did your Uncle Archie who was only sixteen years old,' Ivy said quietly.

'That only left Mum and her brother Lennie. They escaped it. Then along came what we called the Black Plague. The typhoid fever epidemic. That killed Uncle Lennie. So that only left my mother in her family. And now, of her children, there's only me and Frank, the eldest and the youngest,' Louie sighed.

There was a long, sad silence before Ivy spoke.

'Mr James was on the Mission. He saved a lot of lives.'

'White ones, too.'

'He was a doctor and a school teacher,' Ivy resumed. 'Oh, it was terrible. There was no hospital at Barmah then and the Echuca one was full so the Cumera people had to stay in their houses.'

'They had to do the best they could for themselves. When they could they helped each other. A neighbour would sit up with a sick one, all night sometimes.'

'Mr Nelson made hot soup in kerosene buckets and took it around to them. There were no nurses visiting the Mission so the people fended for themselves. People died, one after another.'

'The 'flu and consumption,' Ivy said.

'One time there was a young man who came to Cumera from Warangesda way and he camped over the river on the Victorian side. He was so sick my father went and got him and brought him across to the Mission. The rules were that the people weren't allowed to just take anyone in, but Dad did because he was so ill. They had him in their house, the one that's still on the Mission, and my mother tried to nurse him. Dad wanted to get the doctor out to him, but no way would they allow that. He eventually died. I remember the poor man's mother came down to our house and stood in the bedroom door, trying to stop the doctor from going in when he came to hold the post-mortem. The poor mother cried. It was terrible. She was in a terrible state while it went on. All the blood and things could be seen. She was in a bad way afterwards.'

'They wouldn't get the doctor when he was sick. I know all about that,' Ivy said in disgust.

'They found he died from pneumonia. There was a big Board meeting after that and the manager was sacked. Can't think of his name.'

Ivy had listened to Louie without interrupting the account. She turned to face me.

'People were dying with the same diseases at Coranderrk. My father made the coffins. Lined with white on the inside and black on the outside. He did them good.'

'You'd think they were bought from some funeral parlour,' Louie contributed.' I can remember Grandfather Nelson making the coffins at Cumera. I suppose they'd all be rotted by now. There were so many dying the dray would be going up to the cemetery every day nearly, taking them to be buried.'

'The bell would be ringing. We had it for funerals then. I don't know what they've done with the bell.'

'When anyone died, children were not allowed out to play or make any noise.'

'All silent, eh,' Ivy reverently added.

'After a while instead of the dray, they got the buggies. In those days a long time ago at Cumer, the relations of the dead person had to be held to stop them from getting into the grave with their dead one.'

This conversation brought unpleasant memories of officialdom to both the ladies.

'That Board did some terrible things to our people,' Ivy said.

'It was the law for the Aboriginal people, wasn't it Auntie !'

'Yes. Look at poor old Granny Wentworth. There were four little boys, and a little girl, all related, and she was Granny to them from down Wentworth way where, I think, there was a Station for Aboriginal people. Their mother died, I think. The Board decided to send them away from their own place to live at Cumera. The little girl, Ruby, came first, by herself. After a while they sent her three brothers, Billy, Huey and Tommy. They were put in different homes on the Mission. Billy was taken in by Janet and Tommy went to live with Freddie, and Huey was with Granny Mag and her husband, Henry. The two full-blood boys, Tommy and Huey, fretted for their own, their tribal people from way back at Wentworth.'

'Charlie came after they did. These children were all related but had a different father or mother. This was a long time ago,' Louie told me.

The Joyce family home.

'Long time.' Ivy's eyes were closed for a few moments. I felt her memories were unsettling her and asked if she would like to discontinue the events. It was though I had not spoken. 'Before the First World War. Then one day the steamboat come up again and this time Old Granny Wentworth was on it, and she brought this other little fella with her, named Charlie. She always called him, Mine Boy. The two full-blood boys, Tommy and Huey, didn't seem to be able to take the change from their own people and tribe, and they died.'

'That Board,' Louie burst out as memories flooded back to her of the results of the implementation of the New South Wales Government Protection Acts. 'Makes you wonder why it all came about, Auntie, separating families.'

'That's right,' Ivy said. 'Well, Charlie, Billy and Ruby were real wild ones. We used to go and play with Ruby and she'd get under the table away from us. One of these times, Charlie wasn't around, and they thought he had cleared, but he was up in the pepper tree. After a while, those three wild ones got used to the rest of us kids on the Mission.'

'Granny Wentworth had a little mia-mia on the bank of the river where the barges pulled up to pick up the wool and wheat where it was stacked on the bank at Cumera. The wharf was near the little white house that's there now.'

'She'd be down there, fishin' on the river with her toes, like we said before, and smoking her stumpy pipe'

'Enjoying it, too.'

'She must have missed the other children that died. Mine Boy was always with her then and she loved him. With her 'til the Board took him away from her.' Ivy sounded bitter. 'That broke her heart. They took him up to Sydney and put him to learn in an office or something. She fretted. She fretted over her Mine Boy. She died after they did that to her.'

'Poor Old Granny Wentworth,' Louie said.

'Charlie grew up away from here. Somebody told me that a long time after he did come back once, looking. He married up there and had a large family. Then one day, oh, many, many years later, a man come here looking for Billy. This man was a descendant of Granny's, Mine Boy. He wanted to see other descendants of the children Granny Wentworth had looked after, his own relations. He was a well dressed fella and had a lovely car, and wanted to take me for a drive. It was a nice day and a lot swimming at Sandy Beach. He was a very nicely spoken man. He told me he was a shearer.'

'He was a relation of Granny Wentworth's alright,' Louie confirmed.

'That little Billy is still alive now, and well in his 80s. When he was well, his son used to walk with him to the shops here to cash his cheques. Anyway they sent him away. He doesn't remember much they say and he walks about a lot. A couple of times he went away, then one morning they couldn't find him. They looked everywhere. In the finish they found him up here, laying in the gutter near the ships, in the water, poor old fella. I think he went looking for his son. It's a long time since he was one of Granny's little fellas. She was real nice, wasn't she Louie. So was Old Sophy. She was an old lady round about the time that Granny Wentworth had Mine Boy taken away from her.'

'Sophy could tell when something was going to happen.'

'She did that day when she went down the Mission street and told everyone something was going to happen. Corse, they took no notice of her. 'There's goin' to be somethin' on today,' she told them. 'A red-letter day,' but nobody believed her. She kept calling out, warning the people. My word she was right. It was a red-letter day on Cummeroogunga all right. There was screams and screams.'

'That was the first day they took the girls away,' Louie told me.

'I was there at Cumera when the girls were taken, the first lot that they took.' Ivy emphasized 'first.' 'We were all teenagers.' She pushed her back against the chair straining her body. She drew a deep, long breath, and exhaled slowly.

Ivy was obviously agitated as her memories flooded into her vision. I felt, however, that she and Louie talked about this emotional part of their lives when they were in each other's company, and not in front of an outsider. I therefore did not prompt them with questions. If they wanted to record the part they knew, or had played, in this scarred era of the history of Cumeroogunga which will never lay down in the dust, it was up to these two elderly ladies to make the choice. And they did.

Louise took up the events. 'Bruce Ferguson was the manager. Oh, they've done some cruel things over there at Cumera. Different managers – some good, some bad.'

'Old Sophy worked in the Mission meat shop. She had to clean up in there, wash the floor, all that. This morning while she was working she heard someone talking. Could have been Ferguson talking to the Board people. I don't know, but she heard one of them say, 'It's going to be a red-letter day on Cumera today,' and that's all she heard, but she knew something was wrong and she ran to tell the people. She went down the street tellin' the people. They took no notice of her. She used to walk about lame, she was – guff.'

'Ferguson sent the men off to work in the bush.'

'Yes, before anyone knew the Board people were there with the police, he sent the men down to the sandhill, digging burrows and suckering in the bush. Only one or two of the old men were at home who couldn't work, so after the workers had gone off, the police and the Board people came into the street. My word, Old Sophy's warning was right.'

'They couldn't have got the girls if the men had been there. The old people and the women couldn't stop them,' Louie said.

'I must have been fourteen or fifteen,' Ivy continued. 'I just stood there, watching what was going on, when one of the men called to me. He said he wanted a cook, and I said, 'Oh, I'm too old,' and they didn't get me. Too busy getting others. They went to Florrie's home and told her they had a job for her daughter. She was just a young girl. They took Hilda, and Florrie tried to fight them for her, but they pushed her away onto the ground. One policeman held Hilda while the others tried for Winnie Atkinson, but she was too quick.'

'She got away across the river,' Louie said, giving me the method of Winnie's escape.

'They got Hilda to the lane and shoved her out the back through the cyclone gate near the hill.' Ivy was moving through that day as though it had only just happened. 'By this time there was screaming and crying all over the place. They went after Una then and she tried to fight for herself. All her clothes were torn and she was screaming. They took poor Bella Geish, too. She was standing with her grandfather, Old Ned Joachim and his wife, Annabella. Those old people fought back, but they got Bella into a car. Old Ned tried to get at it with a crowbar.'

'He nearly got it through the window,' Louie said. 'Bella was just visiting her grandparents at Cumera but they took her away.'

'They got three that day, Hilda, Una and Hilda. Took them to Echuca Police Station.'

'What they took the girls for I don't know. They never went out anywhere. They never had anywhere to go.'

'The Board sent these people to the Missions to say they had jobs for the young girls. May Walker was taken up there and some of the Clements too. I don't know where they went from, Moonah or Cumera. I think their father was there and got them back.'

'Was it another time that the Board woman come with another man and a policeman and got Miriam? Was it her they picked up in Moama when she was working for Bertha? Those Board people, you know, they were law.'

'That was the same day. We called Miriam Charles by her nickname, Middy. Bertha and her husband had left Cumera and had their own home in Echuca and Middy worked for Bertha. She sent Middy down to the butcher shop for some meat for dinner. The Board people must have just seen her in the shop and thought they'd take her to the Home – that Cootamundra place. When Miriam didn't get back to Bertha with the meat she went looking for her at the butcher's, and then she found out she had been taken to the police station and they had locked her up there with the other three. She still had the parcel of meat. Bertha went and told Middy's mother where she was ...'

'Middy's mother was Selina but she wasn't at the Mission.'

'And she come to the police and made a fuss, but she couldn't get the girls back, so she stayed there with them all night at the pOlice station. She was with them when they were taken away early next morning. Middy's poor grandmother had to be told that she had gone. She was out at Cumera and didn't know about all this. If she'd been there at the butcher's they'd have had a fight on their hands.'

'If they'd come back to Cumera that night lookin' for more girls they'd have seen some spears! When the men found out what happened they set themselves up in the street at the Mission waiting for them to come back, and they were ready for them,' Louie told me.

'Yes, they were ready and waiting, but they didn't come back that night. They come again other times though, for years. There was May and Nellie Jackson and Margaret Nelson, Marj, Cathy. So many taken by that Miss Lowe to the home. She told the Cumer people she wanted to take some girls to train them to work. Margaret was working at the Moama Police Station then and at that time I was back at Coranderrk. She wrote to me and told me about it.'

'Wasn't she a maid or cleaner there? Domestic work anyway.'

'Yes. She said in her letters that she wouldn't see me anymore. She was going to Sydney, that the Board people were sending her there to learn something. Her mother and father must have believed her, and agreed for Margaret to go and that Miss from the Board took Nellie and Margaret.'

'Girls were taken from Moona and other Missions,' Louie added.

'Just take them. There were three sisters, Caroline, Cathy and Milly Alan, but one of them did not want to go, but because the other two were taken she went with them. Milly was the only one of the three to live. Most of the girls we can't account for. Others died up there. Their parents would not know what happened to them,' Ivy concluded.

'And Nellie and Margaret?' Louie asked.

'They gave those girls as terrible time up there. Cathy was already at that Home when Margaret and Nellie got there and Margaret told me in her letters that Cathy was sick. She was locked in a room on her own and she'd be crying. No-one was allowed to go near her. Margaret said all the dark girls would go around to the window to talk to her. She was hungry. She died in the Home. Nellie and Margaret were sent out to work for people in Sydney. I don't know who they were but Margret wrote to her parents about them but she couldn't say much because they read her letters. We had all her letters where she, 'I can't write much, I'm too tired.'

She was trying to tell her mother and father in-between-the-lines how bad it was but they didn't understand it until it was too late. They worked her too hard at that place and she died. Never saw Cumera again. We never saw her again. After Margaret died they got Nellie back. She told them how bad it was for the girls. She said she never had time to comb her hair. It was all knotted up.'

'There were lots of girls taken off to that Cootamundra Home. Some of the policemen that the Board people had with them didn't want to do that job of taking the girls.'

'I know,' Ivy nodded. 'One of the policemen resigned over it. He told me he couldn't stand it any longer, hearing the screams of the girls and the mothers. He couldn't stand to see what was going on. I knew that years later when he was the manager on Moonacullah.'

'Mission managers, Auntie. They were a mixture. The children had a nickname for Ferguson. They called him Old Firm Stone. There was Danvers, and he wore a big white hat like policemen did in those days,' Louie laughed, and a lively discussion followed involving the merits of the men in charge of Cumeroogunga. They found many incidents to laugh about, but there were some managers without qualities to be admired. 'What about the one that pulled all the good houses down. Lovely little gardens and the picket fences. All gone.'

'He shifted off some of the tribes and he started pulling the houses down.' Ivy turned her head slightly. 'You know, Lou, the strike. Did it before the strike. I wasn't here. I was down at Moonah. Knocked them down and sold the tin he did. In one of the homes he made the son get out of there, poor fellow. Pulled it down over his head. Old Sophy's was the last house they pulled down.'

'The only one left from Maloga is ours,' Louie said. 'That manager got the sack.'

'In gaol over that. Somebody saw him in Sydney after. You know where he was workin' Lou?'

'No.'

Ivy beamed at Louie. 'Cleaning the gutters out,' she pronounced delightedly, and they laughed together at their mental image.

'Him leaving Cumera didn't make everything right' Louie said.

'The Strike. The Walkout. That was terrible. I heard all about it.'

'Never have days like those again. My mother had a bad heart then. Even when an aeroplane flew over the Mission she was that scared.'

Ivy closed the subject of The Strike when she spoke, on side, to me. 'Louie's mother was so upset over the walkout that she died from it.'

'A lot of water has gone under the bridge since those dreadful days,' Louie said. Her voice changed. 'Do you remember the floods we had at Cumera? Were you there then, Auntie Ivy?'

'Which one? When we all had to go down to the sandhills?'

'That's the one. In 1917, the big flood when the water pushed back into the Mission.'

'They say some of the Barmah people cut the embankment,' Ivy said.

'We weren't flooded when we went to bed but in the morning the water was coming in the kitchen. We woke up and stepped in water. We could sail from the Mission out to the sandhills. The people sailed round the Mission streets. We thought it was great and we enjoyed it, us kids. The police hired tents and we all had to camp out on the hills. They had tarpaulins for us. Everyone was happy. Big fires burned around the camps.'

Louie stood up from her chair. 'It's time for us to leave, Auntie Ivy,' she said reluctantly.

She bent over to kiss her friend goodbye.

'Old Cumera,' Ivy whispered, caressing the words. There were tears in her soft-blue eyes.

Chapter Eight

A Song to Remember

'We had some good times when we were little on the Mission,' Louie began. 'We played a sort of 'rounders' but of course we never had proper balls. My great-aunt, Polly Briggs, we called her Granny Polly, she made the balls for us out of torn strips of material. Stitch the pieces together and fill them up. They lasted well. Another game was we had jam tins with string tied to them, then we'd stand on them and trot around the Mission. I remember we called one of the kids Trotter,' she laughed, turning to Ivy. 'He might have been called that because he trotted around the Mission on jam tins.'

'What about when they killed the sheep or beef for the meat supply at Cumera,' Ivy suggested.

'We'd wait and wait there for the gullingun,' Louie promptly replied. 'Everyone seemed to want some. I can remember when one of the boys wanted it so much that he was fighting with Dick, one of the others, while they waited. Dick got his gullingun first and was running off with it when the other boy threw a butcher's knife at him and it went in just above his heel. Straight shot it was! The pair of them, fighting over the gullingun, That's the insides of the sheep,' Louie translated for me. 'Talking about the meat, what about the dampers. You cooked damper in the ashes, Auntie Ivy.'

'Yeah,' she answered with relish.

'I wouldn't mind having a piece now,' Louie said and looked at me. 'You make up something like a scone dough, then you open up your ashes, put the dough in there and cover it over. When you see the ashes all breaking away from the sides you know it's time to turn the damper over.'

'Then when it's finished, get it out and clean the ashes off with a clean cloth and gum leaves, then put butter on, and Ohhhhhh geeeeee, it's lovely. I felt like it the other night, if I could have seen. There was nice ashes in my fire here.'

'We loved the swan eggs in those days. Talk about getting the swans and birds, and their eggs. The men would pack up their boats and go off up the lakes and we'd be waiting for them to come back. They had tea boxes for all the eggs they'd bring home. Can't forget about Old Blue Gum who went after the ducks and swans, and shags, in the river. He'd go in, catch one by its legs and pull it under the water.'

'Blue Gum was Bobby Cooper's nickname. My nephew, Peter Pan, did that , too. He'd swim out to the swans, cover himself with boughs that he held to hide himself. He'd just float along beside the swans and pull them down, then swim back to the bank with them. Big swans, too.' Ivy waited, then murmured thoughtfully, 'I've seen him do it, - um – Peter Pan. The men used gill nets y'know. My brother Peter did, up at First and Second Creeks.'

'If they came to a lagoon you'd see one fella go up on one side with the net and the other one on the other. They'd get the fish. I told you Dad was a fisherman. He made his own nets, and a bark canoe for fishing, and us kids used it to sail around in it. The men lived on Cumera but worked away. My Dad made a living out of fishing. He had men with boats working for him.'

'There were fishing camps all along Barmah Creek in the real early days, with the Cumer men fishing at places like Barnyard, Barmah Creek and Bonny Digger. Rice and Golloway used to go out and buy the fish from the Blackfellows. Remember, Louie?'

'I remember. I remember fishing and camping at Picnic Point and Thistle Bend. My husband was a fisherman, too. He used to go from here to Darlington Point and fish, come back and put the fish on the train to Dalgettys. He made a lot of money.'

'The men would have cork lines in at night, lines across the river and pegged in on each side. They had bells fixed on the lines so that when the fish were caught the bell rang and they'd go out with a light and get them. Sell them to Rice. He was living up on the hill. Old Golloway, too. Both white.'

Joseph Rice, after having tried his luck mining on the Victorian goldfields, established a lucrative fishing business with Aboriginal labour.

'How do you think we got on with the whites when we were young, Auntie Ivy?'

'I think we were alright.'

'The white children went to school at Cumera.'

'Yes, there were the Rices, Nick Verny and ...'

'When they had dances they all joined in, didn't they.'

'Yep,' answered Ivy, smoothing the back of her hand with the palm of the other. She was thinking. We waited patiently without speaking, not wishing to interrupt her thoughts as she sought information locked away for so long in her mind. 'Back in the real early days there were young girls taken to Coranderrk from the Murray, and they got them married straight away at the Mission. I don't know.' Ivy deliberated for a few moments, then said, 'they had children. White children. It might have been for that. Later on Mr Green was in charge and our people liked him, and then Mr Shaw took over from him and he was going to put the fair ones off – out. The people left there on account of these children.'

'Because some of them.'

'Were fairer than others,' Ivy finished. 'That's when the Dunolly family left there and come this way, and your Granny Briggs, Louie. Over the years since then, plenty of families lived at Coranderrk. The Darbys, Hammonds, Mulletts, Hamiltons, lots from different Missions went there, and left there, too. Oh, it's lovely to talk about them, to say their names again.'

In 1893 Agnes Hamilton lived at Cumeroogunga. She wrote to the Secretary of the Board for Protection of Aborigines, Reverend F. Hagenauer, regarding the man she wished to marry. He replied that, as he did not know him, he could not form an idea and reminded Agnes she had not mentioned if the man she fancied was white, black, or halfcaste. Hagenauer warned her to be careful, otherwise she would have to suffer for the rest of her life. It would be wise for her to take the advice given by Mr Shaw.

'We could think of names from all over the place. Old Ernest McGee, the Galways, Joe Walsh, the Coopers and the Atkinsons,' Louie offered.

'Ettie McGee married Billy Galway. His father lived all his life on Thule Station, married Cissy, and that's where Old Galway had his big family, at Thule. When she died, he shifted to Barham with his family.'

'Joe Walsh.'

'He carved beautiful emu eggs. Joe was one of the best. Hilton, his son, still does.'

'You've no idea how many colours within that emu egg they can bring out,' Louie informed me.

'That's true. Now, the Atkinsons and Coopers. At first there was Old Kitty and her children she took to Maloga. The Atknson family – Johnny, Aaron, Lizzie and Eddie, and her Cooper family, Billy, Bobby, Jackie and Ada. There was another Kitty that worked at Moira and she was the mother of Louie's father-in-law.'

'Yes,' Louie said, 'I used to be asked about that.'

Mallee Cooper with the Mayor of Bairnsdale in the 1980s.

'Before I was born Mr James come as a young man, a teacher for the Maloga School, and after a while he married one of his pupils, Ada Cooper, one of Old Kitty's daughters. When the shift to Cumera came he went with the people. Before I left to go to Coranderrk with my father after my own mother died, I went to school in the old school that was brought from Maloga. Mr James taught me.'

'He taught me too, in the old school. He was a strict teacher but kind. He had the school children so good that he could leave us and go home for a cup of tea to their house behind the school. He was a tall, dark man and his wife, Ada, was a midwife.'

Ivy had listened patiently to her friend's account and was ready to expand on the topic.

Hilary Walsh carving emu eggs at the Age Gallery in 1980.

'I can see the houses for the people now, the picket fences, the gardens of flowers, vegetables and fruit trees. Oh, it was lovely. That was when I went to school and Mr James taught me. He did his best with me. He was as nice as they all say he was. A doctor, school teacher and a minister to us, a really lovely person. Other times when I went back to Cumera I went to school sometimes. I went to the old school and the new one. His daughter, Miriam, was teaching, too.' Ivy rested her head back on her chair. 'Shadrach James.' She spoke his name slowly. 'Some of his and Ada's children were Priscilla, Miriam of course, Beccy – she was Rebecca – Ivy, a son named Shadrach, and Archie.'

'One thing about the houses on the Mission, Auntie. They never had baths,' Louie said, sitting up straight.' 'No bathroom, that's what I can't understand. Why is it they never put bathrooms in? We had a big iron tub to use in the winter time and in the summer the river was there, so who'd want to bath in an iron tub when the river was close,' she declared with conviction. But Ivy's mind had moved on into sadder years.

'So many of the people we knew from Maloga and Cumera have died,' Ivy said softly. 'My baby daughter, Vera, died. You see, Johnny Swift had german measles and I felt sorry for him, lying up there in the saltbushes at Cumera and I looked after him. A fortnight after, I had my baby daughter at Coranderrk, but she had the german measles and died three days later.'

The sorrow Ivy felt over the death of her baby so long ago showed in her face and voice. A touching moment that Icould never forget. After some time, Ivy spoke gently.

'I never had any more children.'

I knew this was the time for me to leave these two old friends together. I went to the kitchen, and it was the longest time ever taken to make a pot of tea. When I joined Ivy and Louie they were talking about the songs and hymns they sang in the Mission churches.

Their favourite was, *Shall We Gather At The River*.

Chapter Nine

Work

'Some of those people that lived on the Mission had to walk a long way to go to work,' Ivy remarked.

'There weren't many places close for them to go to. The only places were good distances from home and you'd see the Old People walking way over the hill from the Mission,' Louie recalled easily.

'Managers wanted us to go to work.'

'Us, too, when we were old enough. Now, Old Marky, well,' Louie, with her sentence left in the air continued to me, 'Auntie Ivy tells me, 'your grandfather was married twice' and,'

'Old Marky, we called her,' Ivy interrupted. The mention of her name brought back very happy incidents as both the women giggled together. 'We all liked her. She was real dark.'

'She'd have a little drink and then she would tell us, 'I'm Margaret O'Reilly, John Bull's daughter and I'll go to Warrnambool if I have to walk.'

'Louie's grandfather, Leonard Kerr, was married before he married Louie's granny, Maggie Briggs. He married a woman from Warrnambool and Marky was the result of that.'

Leonard Kerr married Isabella from Lake Condah in 1875. Their eight-day-old baby girl is buried in the Coranderrk Cemetery.

Ivy continued. 'Oh, poor Marky. I can picture her and poor Auntie Polly Briggs in the rain, going for wood.'

'I can just hear them, you know,' Louie said.

'The women used to go out in the dray and get all the wood and bring it home.'

'With big draft horses.'

'Think nothing of it at Cumera, yeah,' Louie added thoughtfully.

'Auntie Eadie went out doing washing , summer and winter,

and those women wouldn't get the pay then that they get now. Poor old lady, crippled she was. She got something wrong with her leg. Remember where she had to go to work? She walked from the Mission right away up to Tinklers. You'd see her go over the hill.'

'That place is burnt down now,' Louie said. 'She'd walk right way out there, summertime, didn't matter. She'd go there and wash. Eadie Elliot.'

'Married Bob Elliot. Eadie was Old Sophy's mother. She was a hard worker, too. Worked around different places. Old Sophy was a great singer. She always sang in the Church. She was a real nice lady. Married Billy Briggs and one of her children is Kenny. His wife is related to Peppers. I met a Pepper fella from Orbost. Quiet man.'

'Some of the mothers carried their babies on their backs at the Mission. Made it easier to do their work and get about.'

"You can see them in the museum in Melbourne, photos of them. Annie Hamilton and Lizzie Barber are there with babies on their backs,' Ivy said.

'I remember Lizzie, but when I knew her she was a real old lady.'

'Oh, they'd put them in the blanket and tie them in here, eh?' and Ivy demonstrated, meeting with Louie's approval. 'One tied on the back, one toddling and one in her arms.'

'Oh yes, we've seen them like that,' Louie answered, dismissing that subject. 'Where else did you work, Auntie Ivy?'

'When Clarkes were at Moira I walked there from Cumera, and I worked there for a long time. Another place I walked to was old Mrs Johnson's to do the washing. One time she wanted me to stay to do the ironing and I wouldn't. She had a horrible bed, the spring was no good and I wouldn't sleep in it – not at Mrs Johnson's place! I walked home that night.'

'Before we went to Cumera to live I can remember my mother washing the floors over – dirt floors – when we lived out along the Murray River. We were happy there I tell you. When I first went to work, that was at Yarroweyah for Tweddles, I got ten shillings a week. I had ten cows to milk and do the house as well.'

'Yarroweyah' or Yarrawonga. Yarroweyah, on the Murray, west of Yarrawonga.

'A job one of the men had at Cumera was being a Black Policeman,' Ivy ventured. Leaning over to push Louie's arm she continued. 'I can still see Herbie Nicholls now. He had real big eyebrows. He had a baton, eh, and he had leggings on. I can picture him just as he was.'

'Oh, he reckoned he was a real policeman,' Louie said.

'Some of the boys played up. They'd be digging in the gardens; doing all sorts of things; flirting. Sometimes Herbie could be after the wrong ones.'

Back: Stewart Murray and David Anderson.
Front: Bob Egan and Sir Douglas Nicholls, 1983.

Louie nodded vigorously, laughing.

'He had some of them up for sheep stealing, eh Louie?'

'He did,' she replied, still laughing, and they talked and joked about the trivial misdeeds of some of the youths, and Herbie's work to keep order.

'They had a little place up the back of the Mission where they would lock them up till the police come for them. Some of them would get into Herbie, eh, Louie.'

'Oh dear.' Louie was not inclined to enlarge on that issue. 'The Old People believed in punishment for the boys when they played up. They, what they called it, smoked them. Put in a bag and held near the smoke of the fire. It happened on the Mission, too. The young ones were told the old stories and shown different things by the old men, the things they did before they were taken onto the Missions. They frightened the children about Numbak-bul , the one that gets you.'

Ivy was not to be distracted.

'Herbie's job was to stop the boys from playing up. Somebody asked me once if his son, Doug, was the first born at Cumera. I told them there were a lot before him. Doug's own mother, Florrie, was the first born at Maloga Mission. She was Old Kitty Atkinson's granddaughter. I was on the Mission at Cumera when Doug was born. I was playing in the gutter when Dr Stone came with his bag and went in to Florrie in her house. Poor Florrie, oh, she had a hard time. Herbie Nicholls was walkin' up and down outside, up near the pepper trees near the store where their little place was. The doctor came out and he said to Herbie, 'It is a boy,' and Herbie went in and talked to Florrie.'

'And now he is Sir Douglas Nicholls,' Louie declared.

'Did you say you'll be calling in on the way back to Echuca to see Freddie Walker, Lou?' A nod confirmed it. 'He's about the same age as Doug. They were in short pants at the same time,' Ivy recalled. Years after, I come up on the train from Deniliquin, and they were working on the line at Moira.'

Captain Reg Saunders and Stewart Murray, 1989.

Chapter Ten

The Old Days with Freddie Walker and Louie Atkinson

'We like talking about the old days,' Freddie assured me. 'Only too happy to. I'm descended from Edward Walker. His son, Freddie, married Sarah, and they were the first married couple to live on Maloga after it became the Mission. Daniel Matthews brought a lot of dark people there. He took Freddie Walker, Sarah and little son, and Frank Barber, Lizzie and little boy Frank, all to Maloga from Red Bank, called Mathoura now. They came to Maloga from all over.'

'Yes, Auntie Ivy has told me about people, and where they came from, that I didn't know about,' Louie said.

'When they come to Cumera they got out of their old ways. They worked them into the white society. Not many left to talk to now. I suppose you know your grandfather, Leonard Kerr, came from Wyuna, Louie. My father told me about him. He was around the white Curr family. He was well-known around as far as Tongala. Old Leonard reared his family at Cumera. He was on the wagon for rations and had to go from the Misson to Moama and back and it was a two-day trip then. He had four horses pulling the wagon.'

Freddie pulled a pouch of tobacco from his pocket and rolled his own. He puffed away for several moments.

'My father, Herb, married Florrie Hamilton. I was born on the bank of the Murray River at Cumera. When I was a little fella we shifted from Cumera to Barmah. The old man was working on the mill. I went to school at the Mission and Doug Nicholls was there in my time. Mr James had a chemist shop and he worked under Dr Stone at Cumera, and he had two teachers under him at the school. My mother was a midwife at the Mission.'

'That's Auntie Florrie. We all knew her. She'd say to us after we'd had a baby, 'Not a foot outside that bed for ten days.'

'That's the way it was then. She worked under Dr Grahram and he wouldn't come out to the Mission unless she said for him to come. Mum's people come from Coranderrk. Auntie Ivy knows my mother's mob. Dad had relatives down at Coranderrk. He was related to Granny Jemima. The Wandins are related to my father and the Terricks. Old John Terrick and his wife called each other Honey. I called the men 'uncle' when I stayed with Old Granny Jemima at Coranderrk.'

'Auntie Ivy said they nicknamed you Butcher Boy because you wore a blue suit or blue apron or something.'

Freddie drew on his cigarette, smiled, and explained the 'something.'

'When I was a little fella W.T. McAlister took his horses to the show and I remember I had a badge on so I was allowed to go in. He was on the Board for Aborigines and he always had Aboriginal people working for him and always paid them. I knew Ernie Shaw. The Shaws had been in charge there, and I knew the Roberts when they were in charge. Some of our people on the station were the Mulletts, Davis's, Pop Young, he went away in the army, Old Billy Russel, Alec Taylor. While I – we – were at Coranderrk, we had to get permission to go into town. Every Saturday horse-drawn carriages full of tourists would come out for a couple of hours to buy boomerangs, shields, baskets and anything else our people made. Lanky Manton and his wife, Annie, and Alf and Lizzie Davis were there then. All dead now.'

'Who else do you remember from Cumera, Freddie?' Louie asked.

'Maggie and Henry Nelson, and they had a family. Had a store, too. There was your father, a successful fisherman, Lou. He employed the men, paid them so much a pound for their catch. He was a bike river as well. We had good athletes there at Cumera. Professional. Lynch Cooper won the Stawell Gift and Eddie Briggs was in the Gift – he was Minnie and Alec's son. Minnie was an Atkinson. There were a lot of sportsmen that have come from the Mission, and their children grew up to be footballers and coaches. We had three football teams there at one time. One of the Weston boys played, a relation of yours. I could name a lot of the players.'

'The men worked on the Cumera land,' Louie urged.

'Yes, at one time we had sixty-five draft horses, 2000 acres, and a lot of it in crops. The men had 40-acre blocks and were paid wages. We'd stack the wheat on the bank and the barges took it to Echuca. You know, there'd be kids teeming about the place, but I never knew of one getting drowned. It must have been an instinct with the little ones, but the older ones did look after them. When the river was low we'd cart gravel from it for the Mission streets and paths.'

Fred Walker and Louise Atkinson, 1983.

'Auntie Ivy said you and Doug worked on the railway lines.'

'We were only about fifteen years old when we got in with Bill Pearce and the Bettson Brothers from Echuca, and we worked on the Balranald line when it was going through. Dam sinking and channelling.' He knocked the ash from his cigarette. 'You know, Louie, I learned to make boomerangs when I was a kid at Coranderrk, and now my son, Colin, makes them. He watched my father making them. But, strangely enough, I never seen the Old People strip a canoe.' He sounded as though he couldn't believe it himself. Louie shook her head. 'It was a long time before I ever saw a canoe taken from a tree.'

‘There’s not too many of the old scarred trees about now to see,’ Louie said. She watched Freddie roll another cigarette while he talked about this one particular tree.

‘I was in the bush working for the Forest Commission and I was the only dark fellow amongst the men. We worked in pairs, and this day Paul Rice and me felled this tree and he said he’d strip a canoe. He made some wedges and took the bark off, tapped it off. It took about six of us to carry it.’

Freddie examined his cigarette, pulled some loose tobacco from the top and put a match to the cigarette. He drew on it, lifted his head and blew out a thin trail of smoke.

‘That is the only one I have ever seen stripped. And it was a white boy who did it!’

Canoe Tree on the Murray, Echuca, 1982. (Courtesy Jack O’Mullane)

There was a silence for a while until Freddie began talking softly and sadly to Louie about the lost arts of their people, of the few trees that stood with the scars showing where their ancestors had used the bark for their every need. He was proud that his son, Colin, made and sold boomerangs. He turned directly to me.

‘The Old People showed us a lot of things. They talked to us, told us about the early days. I've often wondered, though, why they never talked about our people with cancer. It must be the food that causes it now. Most of the children of those Old People have gone. Not many left to talk to now. There's Ivy, Louie here, and me, about these parts.'

Louie and I left Freddie Walker's home and returned to Echuca after being with Ivy, Louie and Freddie during July, 1983.

I was destined never to see Freddie again, or to listen to Ivy Sampson's lively experiences and, alternatively, her heart-rending stories.

Ivy died in 1984 and she rests not far from her baby in the sands on the hill, at her beloved Cumera.

Freddie Walker joined the Old People himself in 1986.

Chapter Eleven

Recollections of Mick Kelsall

Mick Kelsall grew up in Echuca and Moama, and as a young man he worked with his father on the Murray River during the 1930s. Author of *A Riverman's Story*. As he is non-Aboriginal, his recollections are pertinent.

'My Dad and I worked on the outrigger barges that brought the redgum logs to the sawmills at Echuca. This method was developed because the redgum logs will not float. The barges were towed by paddle-steamers upstream, then dropped off at the landings. They'd be loaded then by the barge.

'Where the logs were loaded upstream, and below the Moira Lakes, the Aborigines fished with their drum nets while the Murray was high and therefore the water was muddy. On one particular day two of the Aboriginal men paddled their flat bottomed dinghy alongside the barge and called out to us, 'Do you want some fish?' Sure, we wanted some fish. It would be much better than the greasy corned beef that we had to eat because it was the only meat that would keep for any length of time. They gave us the fish, and Dad told them there was hot tea in the billy down below, and cake in the tin on the top of our 'soapbox cupboard.'

'Well, they left the fish with us and went down below for tea and cake and when they came up on deck again they thanked us and went paddling off downstream. That night, after we'd eaten the feed of fish they'd given us, Dad thought he'd top it off with some cake. He was in for a surprise. It was all gone. A whole week's supply of cake. They'd eaten the lot. That was understandable because cake was not an item of food the Aborigines had in their diet. Next time we made sure some got put aside for us.

'After our barge passed the Barmah punt, drifting downstream with a heavy load, we'd see an odd humpy on the New South Wales side, then the Cumeroogunga Mission where the bank of the Murray River had a gentler slope. We knew a whole community lived in there, and usually a lot of the people would come down to see the barge pass by. One of the delights of drifting through the Mission was to hear the singing of the kids and the teenagers. They had a fondness for country-western music. On each side of the river they seemed to yodel out to each other, the echo coming back through the gumtrees.

'On a few occasions the river remained high enough for us to continue barging well into the summer. On one of these particular hot days my father and I were on deck, getting whatever breeze there was about. The sun was blazing and reflecting off the water and I remember the cicadas were trying to deafen us, and each other, with their chirping. As we drifted through Cumeroogunga a couple of the boys from the Mission who'd been watching us from the bank, threw off their clothes and jumped into the river and swam out to our barge. They pulled themselves up and stood on the logs, drifting with us and waving to their little mates.

'Next minute the logs and outriggers were swarming with children. Yelling, duck-diving, pushing each other off the logs into the water, racing one another, laughing, somersaulting off the outriggers, calling out, having a great time – and completely ignoring our presence.

'From the river we could see some of the places the Mission people had to live in. Saplings for the framework covered by some iron and flattened kerosene tins. Yet the kids played happily around. We'd see the boys kicking a football around made of tied up newspapers. A few of the older boys could put on an exhibition of boxing, a sport they all loved. The diet of the Mission people consisted mainly of rabbit and fish, although the Government did dole out some supplies like flour and sugar.

'As Moama was a small town there was some difficulty fielding a footy team good enough to get near the top of the competition in those days. The club needed skilled players so they imported some of the talented men from Cumeroogunga. These Aborigines meant as much to the Moama Club as the Krakow brothers do to North Melbourne. There was Maurie Charles, weaving his way towards the goals; the skills of Ortie Weston; full back Freddie Walker; and Dowie Nicholls, Doug's brother. Like the rest of the footy team, they never received any payment. They just played for the love of the game.

'Times were hard in the 1930s and jobs were hard to get. There was one monotonous job that was shunned by most men, and that was cutting thistles some miles out from Moama. Dowie Nicholls and some of his mates took it on, but not one of them had a watch, nor did they have the money to buy one. Dowie solved the problem by bringing a large alarm clock with him from his home. He threaded the belt of his trousers through the ring on the top of the clock, then buckled up the belt on his trousers. Every time Dowie took a swing at a thistle the bell on the clock 'dinged.' That caused a lot of jokes and laughs amongst his mates and Dowie joined in with the fun.

'Only recently I was with some artists and our painting group had an exhibition of their work. I was wandering around having a look when I suddenly saw a painting that jolted me back sixty years. It was the Firebrace house in old Moama. The Aboriginal family lived there and I knew their children went to the Moama State School because their eldest daughter was there when I was. The father was a well respected man and so was his family. My cousin, just a lad then, worked with him, or I should say, Mr Firebrace taught him the job of driving horses and scooping out a dam on a property out of the town. He enjoyed being with Mr Firebrace.

The Firebrace Home in 1986, used in the film All the Rivers Run.

'When the Firebrace family left Old Moama their house was rented to various people, including my aunt and her family. Many times I slept under it's roof. I can still recall it's high gable. I remember the levee bank against the fence around the property to keep out the floodwaters that sometimes invaded the lower end of the town.

'The Firebrace home became well-known because it was the house used for the hero and heroine to settle into after their marriage in the television saga, *All The Rivers Run*.'

Chapter Twelve

The Sand Hill

When I visited Mrs Louisa Atkinson in the May of 1986, she was still feeling the great loss of Ivy Sampson and, more recently, Freddie Walker. Now, another nephew of Ivy's had died. He was Rupert Cooper, seventy-five years old, and to be buried at Cummeroogunga the next day.

We sat in the lounge room and our conversation was enlivened with photographs of family, friends and places, and Louise's happy instances accompanying the pictures. She brought out her own Birth Certificate and handed it to me to read. Her father, Richard Joyce, was a labourer and born at Narrandera, New South Wales, and her mother, Constance Kerr was born at Maloga, Victoria. She was 22 years old and Richard was 24 when they married. Louisa was born on 30 October, 1908, at Cummeroogunga Aboriginal Station, Moama. The informant was C. Joyce and the witness was Louisa Briggs. 'We always spelt the Mission, Cummeragunja,' Mrs Atkinson said, pointing to the word.

'My son, Leo, and Jessie McGee are doing up the cemetery,' she told me. 'They've been working there for some weeks now and some of the other residents out there have been helping them. Now, of course, there's preparations going on for poor Rupert.'

Louie ran her hand down her leg, rubbing it carefully.

'I'm not as good as I was, but I can walk about, and that's a good thing. We could go out to Cumera if you like – 'cause we won't be seeing poor Auntie Ivy at her place this time. Ah. She loved those talks we had. Me too,' she barely whispered.

We did go out to Cummeroogunga, and as we drove through the first gate I thought of Old Moolbung and his rattling tin in the gumtree. We met Jessie and Leo in the village.

'We've come to see the cemetery,' Louie greeted them. 'You'll take us out?'

It was cold, bleak and windy out there on the hill as Jessie and Leo guided us along the paths, across the grass, and around the mounds of earth, sometimes in rows, others solitary.

'The mounds cover some of our people,' Jessie explained. 'We want to have a plaque for each family section with their names clearly showing.' As we walked further across the cemetery Louie dropped back to walk slowly with Leo, talking to him all the time.

Jessie told me the names of the families grouped together. 'You'll understand it better if we go back to the entrance,' and we retraced our steps, moving amongst the graves. I felt every one of those buried there knew we were on that sand hill.

'Here at the gate coming into the cemetery is the Joyce family, Auntie Louie's father's side, and the Kerrs, again Auntie Louie's people, are not far from them.' Jessie moved a little ahead. 'Annie and Clarrie Atkinson are a bit further on, and Dan Atkinson and family are near the fence. Over there is Gladdie Nicholls, Sir Doug's wife, the one with the logs around it.'

As we walked, Jessie pointed to different family blocks, calling their names to me above the wind, and as she did, minute episodes of their lives flashed across my mind discovered in official record but more often given to me in Ivy's excited voice, and Louie's happy tones, or Freddie's soft and gentle words.

'The families of James, Muir, Briggs, Walker – Uncle Fred is here where the fresh flowers are, then there where Jack and Bella Cooper are, and Tommy and Audrey are up the top.' We continued walking up the hill. 'There is Henry Button's grave with the old headstone.' Just then Louie's voice floated on the wind to us. 'The Jacksons are near there, too.'

'Auntie Ivy asked me for a favour,' Jessie said as we walked across the hill. 'I'll show you where she is buried. One day not long before she died, she told me of her baby girl. I didn't know she had a child at all. Auntie Ivy said to me, 'Where the May bush grows is where she is. Will you keep her grave nice?.' I told her I would. I knew where the May bush was, but it had died. So I knew then where the baby was buried. Auntie Ivy's little baby girl is there,' Jessie pointed, 'on the hill above Auntie Ivy. Auntie is near her husband, Bertie Sampson.'

'Back from Baby Sampson's grave is the place where the ground was prepared for my brother, Colin, but they found someone else there and no-one knows who now. There are a lot like that, just mounds, or flat ground. Auntie Ivy told me a lot of the names and where they are buried. Not far over is my grandmother, Ester Dunolly, and Auntie Ivy's brothers, Peter and Dave. Some of the Dunolly graves are flat.' We moved on a little. 'Another of her brothers is here, Tommy, and there is Rosie, his wife. Near Auntie Ivy are her nephews, Peter and Tom Dunolly, her niece Jessie Cooper and husband, Andy.'

I thought of Ivy's talk with Louie about Jessie and the family photographs when Ivy had said, 'Jessie must have felt herself getting dying when she told me about them photos she was looking after,' and Louie had replied, 'They say you know when it's time.' Ivy agreed and said, 'You can feel it, eh, coming. Um.'

Jessie McGee pointed. 'There's Louisa McGee, who was Auntie's niece, and Colin her husband, my brother. All these related. From here we can see the Bamblett section, Nelson, Morgan, - '

'That's the Morgan section up there on the hill where the wattle tree was,' Louie called.

Fred Walker's grave.

There are lots of graves here on the top of the hill,' Jessie said. 'There was an old wattle tree and a grave inside the wrought iron fence but I don't know who that is now. I'll tell Nan [Louie] and she might remember.' We walked back to Louie, and Jessie asked about the grave near the wattle.

'That's Dinah Morgan. She married a Kerr. She was Richard Kerr's mother. I don't know where her husband was buried.'

A monument had been placed on the rise of the hill and I stood with Jessie and Louie, reading the words:

> This monument is erected by relatives and friends to the memory of Our Beloved People. They being dead. Yet Speaketh.

Indeed they were speaking, their voices still being heard through their descendants. Jessie turned form the monument and looked around.

'Oh,' she said, spreading her arms out, taking in the whole area. 'I'd like to have the cemetery look like a garden. That's what we're trying to do, Leo and I. We're going to plant roses each side of the gate. We're going to clear off the berry bushes and we'll have benches there for the people to sit down. Some get very tired when they're old.'

Jessie pointed to several tree. 'Those old dead gums we'll cover with morning glory. I'll go into Nan's and get some of that.' She looked back over her shoulder. 'I am going down where the old cemetery used to be, at Maloga. All the headstones are pushed up against the fence there, and I'm going to have a look one day and I will get the readings off them.' Then in a worried tone she added, 'They're on somebody's property now.'

As we walked through the cemetery towards the gate Jessie pulled at a blackberry bush.

'We're getting a bigger tractor soon and that will get those out quickly. It'll really look good. You know, back years ago, they built their own coffins.' We caught up with Louie and Leo and Jessie continued. 'When I was small I remember they kept the black wood for the coffins in the gaol house. Us kids would see all these coffin boards in there and we were frightened. We wouldn't go near.'

'Grandfather Henry Nelson made the coffins,' Louie told Jessie.

Leo walked along beside me describing future plans and projects. 'There are 1500 acres on Cumera now and eighty-six people live here. There will be a boundary fence soon, and a sign is going up at the front gate, Cummeroogunga Village. It's being considered that lucerne and strawberries should be put in, and a nursery.'

Descendants of the Patton and Bamblett families in 1980 at Dight's Falls, were Dixon Patton and Richie Bamblett. Richie is in the photo.

'We had tomatoes and wheat here years ago,' Jessie said.

'The men are building a big fish hatchery down on the bend near the big trees towards Barmah,' Leo said. 'A Community Hall will be built and there are going to be playgrounds for the children and a B.B.Q. area straight across from the school.'

'We're going to get a pre-school back here at Cumera. I'm going to be the teacher. I am a pre-school teacher. Leo and I are the caretakers of the school that's here now.'

'We've had four new brick homes built and the people are setting out the gardens and lawns. We've renovated an old house and it is now the Hostel for the elderly people.'

'The Old Maloga house where Mum was born is to be renovated and used as a museum,' Louie smile, very pleased with the latest suggestion to see her home in its former condition.

Leo walked with us to the Hostel where Lorna Walker showed me through the nicely furnished, warm and comfortable, five bedroomed home.

I've been here for nearly four months,' Lorna explained. 'I'm just looking after the place temporarily, till we get someone permanent.'

She and Louie introduced me to the women and men in the lounge room and we chatted about their families and where they had come from in the early day.

'I'm a Charles.' Lorna volunteered. 'My father-in-law is here, Eddie Walker. He is eighty-eight.'

'Freddie's brother,' Louie told me, interrupting her conversation with one of the ladies, then she quickly picked up the threads again regarding a recent illness. Suddenly everyone joined in, singing the praises of Old Man Weed. They all swore by the benefits of using Old Man Weed.

'A relation of mine lost all her hair when she had a blood disease,' Lorna told us. Doctors' tablets did no good, so she went onto Old Man Weed. That cured her.'

After we left the Hostel we drove and walked around the gravelled streets of the village, over the speed traps, noting the parking bays, the splendid new homes, and Leo picking up one piece of chocolate wrapper that had dared to mar the street.

When we had driven out from Cummeroogunga, Louie spoke.

'I've been many a time across the river from the Mission on the Barmah punt. It was there at the time of the 'walk out' from Cumera. We didn't cross the bridge into Barmah to get into Victoria. We returned along the road to Moama and crossed the river there back into Victoria to get to Echuca. Y'know, if anyone is sick Leo brings them in to the doctor or hospital. He takes me shopping. He pushes the trolley around for me.' Louie talked about the Firebrace family, their home and their store. 'Poor Arthur. When Bertha died he couldn't live there and he went to Melbourne.'

Back at Louie's home, we sat drinking tea in the lounge room which was overflowing with photographs and ornaments that filled the atmosphere with memories for her. She told me of her marriage.

'I'd been married to Frank for thirty years when he died. That was a long time ago. It's twenty-nine years since he died,' and her thoughts were her own for a few minutes, then she talked about Maloga.

'A long time ago the Matthews house burned down at Maloga. Now there's a farm there and somebody said they were growing tobacco. The sad part is, some-one didn't know the cemetery was there and ploughed it in.' This did distress Louie.

'The first burial place is at Maloga and our people would like a bit of the ground there, near where the old pine tree was. That's where the burial ground is. We could put a plaque there to say where the Aborigines are buried. They say there are a lot of the headstones still there at Maloga.'

Louise Atkinson's display of her Aboriginal weapons in her home.

Louie looked at her hands clasped tightly in her lap. She spoke so softly that I was not sure whether I was meant to hear.

'After you've been out to Cumera it brings memories of people and places. You think of the hundreds buried in the sandhill there at the Mission. And Maloga.'

She held up several photographs, saying, 'I have thirty-seven grandchildren and I'm not sure just how many great-grandchildren, but I know I've got one great-great-grandson.' She touched the photographs, moving them around with her finger.

'I think of what these little ones will never see, or do, like we did when we were small.' Her voice trailed away. 'Taking bark from the trees to put the meat on. Washing ourselves in basins made from the bark off the trees.'

Louie smiled suddenly, and the melancholy expression on her face and in her voice vanished. Her eyes brightened and she laughed.

'I can remember watching the emus being cooked on the camp fire.'

Chapter Thirteen

A Chance Meeting

Eileen Kenny, the daughter of Phillip and Ethel Pepper, accompanied me in October 1987, on a research trip which included Charlton on the Avoca River. Eileen's parents had both died, Ethel in 1984 and Phillip in 1985.

Coming into Charlton, a roadside board heralded The Festival of Country Music. The traffic thickened until, by the time we saw the recreation centre in the park, there were crowds of people walking about, talking in groups or pouring into the park.

The town is 280 kilometres north-west by rail from Melbourne. Pastoral and agricultural country, and the secondary industry is flour milling. Lieutenant Charlton was a member of Thomas Mitchell's party that crossed the Avoca River in 1836 at the site of the present Charlton.

'Country singing that sign says,' Eileen read. 'I love country and western. Must be a big do on here.'

We walked into the newsagency, browsing, buying a few cards and the local paper. Eileen gave me a shove and hissed through clenched teeth, 'There's Jimmy Little. Look, over there,' and with her head averted she shot her eyes towards a tall, well-built and smartly dressed man. 'That's him all right. He had his band playing at Bairnsdale for Aboriginal Week.'

Her father had told me so much about Jimmy Little the Aboriginal Singer, and had given me a tape, that I wanted to meet him. Eileen was nervous about speaking to him and eventually he heard us talking and arguing in undertones about which one of us would approach him. He turned around to face us.

'Eileen Pepper.'

'You recognize me?'

'Of course I do,' he said, and gathered her in a big hug. 'I remember you when you were only a little girl. Your mum and dad, and your brothers , too.'

Eileen introduced me to Jimmy and his wife. He asked about my writing and where I had been to search out the Old People and Aboriginal History. When I mentioned Cummeroogunga he took my arm.

'Let's get out of the shop. I'd love to talk to you about Cumera. I wish I could spend more time with you both but I'm a guest here for the Country Singing Festival and I have to go soon.'

We all paid for our purchases and stood outside on the pavement, talking:

'I was born under a tree on Cummeroogunga Mission. Fifty years ago. My mother was Frances McGee and she was the baby of the McGee family. I am her eldest child. I went to school at Cumera where I had a lovely time, and I can remember watching the barges coming down the river with the wheat and the wool. I was seven years old when I left Cumera. My Dad's Mission was Walliga Lake and he took our family back there, so I grew up mostly with his people. I can remember watching him one time, cutting timber in Gippsland.

Every now and again I'd come back to Cumera to see Mum's people. I remember going fishing, or just standing on the river bank with the rest of the kids; diving for mussels; going across the river in the punt to Barmah; rowing the boat over to Barmah and bringing the punt back. I have fond and vivid memories of Cumera Mission.

There were visits to Koondrook and Barham where my aunties and uncles were on my mother's side. My mother's sister married a Galway so the Galways are my first cousins. There was Auntie Bella McGee who married Uncle Bill Atkinson. So many names – Briggs, Charles – all one big happy family. Their children are spread all over.

I've regretted not being able to grow up with them more. A part of me is in Victoria and a part of me in New South Wales. Because I had to get my career going. So you make sacrifices in family circles, to go from the community into the commercial, which is what I did. I knew I couldn't sing around Kyabram and Echuca. I had to sing in the entertainment capital of Australia – Sydney, he laughed, 'for more people to enjoy Jimmy Little. If I hadn't done that,' he put his arm around Eileen, 'I wouldn't have got down to Bairnsdale.

'What time did you finish at the Bairnsdale Ball?' Eileen asked.

'Three o'clock in the morning and we left at eight to go back, as we had work in Sydney. Big trip. Travel is a beautiful education and it's a lovely way of keeping in touch with all our family and friends. But a lot of us can't travel as much as we'd like.'

'We've only just started to travel,' Eileen told Jimmy. 'The kids are off our hands now.'

'The beauty of it is to be able to rear your children up to adulthood, then you have the rest of your life to enjoy the things you had put aside. That's what I'm doing now.'

After saying goodbye to us, Jimmy Little put his hand out to his wife and they walked away together.

Eileen Kenny and Jimmy Little at Charlton in 1987.

Chapter Fourteen

The Indian from the Mauritius Isle

The versatile man who never goes unmentioned in conversations about Maloga and Cummeroogunga is one commonly known as Thomas Shadrach James. His great-grandson, Greg James, and his wife, Terry, welcomed me into their home to meet Greg's mother, Roma, in 1986.

Greg James, a Vietnam Veteran. Former VFL umpire, retired from the game in 1985.

'There has not been enough written about my grandfather,' Roma said, directing me to a chair. 'He was a brilliant man. He studied medicine and theology. He was a teacher, a chemist and a herbalist. According to what we know, Grandpa James came to Australia from Mauritius on a freight boat. Worked his way out here. He met a young man at the wharf who was very good to him and helped him when he first landed. They became friends. This man's name was James, and as Grandpa found his own surname was difficult for the people he met to pronounce or spell, he took the name of the person who had helped him, James.'

'Now, according to other family history, Grandpa James was born in Mauritius and he went to England first where he studied medicine, but somewhere he contracted typhoid fever and this left him with slightly shaking hands, and his head used to nod a bit, so he couldn't practice as a doctor. He went to Tasmania and bought a chemist shop, and when he sold that it was then that he came to Melbourne, still in his twenties. He studied and became a school teacher. We know he spoke French, English and Tamil.

When Daniel Matthews had Maloga Mission going he needed a school teacher. Grandfather James knew about Maloga and offered to help, and in 1881 he was appointed as the teacher. He was in his late twenties when he married Ada Cooper who was eighteen years old. Her mother was Kitty, a full-blood, and she had eight these eight children, Atkinsons and Coopers. Strange things happened in those days, and no one knows for sure what went on. Ada and Thomas were married in May, 1885. Later in the year Old Kitty died of tuberculosis.

'Grandmother and Grandfather James had eight children. The three sons were Archie, Shadrach and Thomas. Whey my father, Thomas, was a baby, Grandpa went home to Mauritius for a holiday. He'd wanted Grandma Ada to go too, but she wouldn't because of baby. Grandpa sent a trunk of clothes back to her from Mauritius. While he was there he passed his own brother, Ebenezer, in the street without knowing him.

'My father was the youngest of Thomas Shadrach's and Ada's children. My mother was one of the Hamilton sisters. Freddie Walker's mother was Florrie, another of the sisters. When my Mum and Dad married, they lived at Cumera with their parents. I can remember my mother talking about the times when he was young and girls were taken from the Mission. They took the boys at times, too, so that when the troopers came to take the children off them her mother, Theresa Hamilton, hid her and her brother, Dick. I think she said up the chimney inside their house. Grandmother Theresa only had the two children then.

'They used to come down and take children away to be domestics or to work for the squatters who were setting up homes on the land. A lot of the dark kids went to New South Wales and ended up in homes, different homes. The mothers never heard of them again. But I never found out why they took them. Because it was just the law that time, I suppose.

'Grandma Ada was a midwife at Cumera. The saying is that over the years that the James lived on the Mission, Grandpa delivered children pulled their teeth, married the, and he buried them. I've been told he studied theology, too. There's a lot of well-known people that he did teach at Cumera, including Sir Doug Nicholls and Margaret Tucker. He was teacher to the Matthews children and other white children that went to the Cummeroogunga school.'

Margaret Tucker, MBE. Born at Warangesda Mission in 1904. She also lived at Moonaculla and Cummeroogunga. Margaret was thirteen years old when she and her sister, May, were taken from Cumera. No authority for this action was given by her mother.

'When Rebecca, one of Ada and Shadrach's daughters, was a young woman, she had a degree from the Conservatorium of Music in Melbourne, and she taught music. Aunt Beccy and Grandpa walked for miles around from Cumera to take church services. Sometimes they were lucky and had the use of a horse and gig. She played the organ or piano for the singing. Now she is elderly and not well and has to be cared for. She talks about the times when she was very young and living at Cummeroogunga with her parents and brothers and sisters. Aunt Beccy was a very beautiful woman.

'Once when I saw her and asked how she was going she said, "Oh, my throat's sore, darling," Terry said. I asked her what was the trouble and she told me, "Oh, it's terrible. We had to go to Echuca to have my tonsils out." I knew she must have been back in the past so I told Greg's mother.

'Grandpa did take Auntie Beccy to Echuca to have her tonsils out. They went in by horse and cart. She sat in a chair while this chap took her tonsils. He had this little thin that he put down her throat that had two little blades on it and a little cup. He just sliced the tonsils off and they dropped into the cup. That's how they had treatment in those days.

'They had a lot of consumption on the Mission at the turn of the century. There was one particular woman they had taken to Echuca Hospital but she was sent home to Cumera to die. Grandpa James cured her with herbs and she lived to be a grandmother. There were such a lot of people that the doctors couldn't do anything more for, and back they'd be sent to the Mission. Grandpa would get to work on them, and he often saved their lives.

'Because the people could not go into Echuca in the real old days, they used a lot of olive oil. If they were sick they'd be dosed up with it. If they had sore ears, it was put in. The people died of simple things like spider bites and measles. If anyone had a deep cut they'd just sew it up with a piece of twine and throw some kerosene over it.

'Another of Nana and Grandpa's daughters was Ivy. She was a very slim, beautiful young woman, and when she was seventeen she married a white man. He wanted to go to the Northern Territory to work on the Aboriginal Missions, so she went with him, but we think the people there didn't want Auntie Ivy amongst them because she wasn't one of them. After a while her husband wanted one of the Aboriginal women on the Mission. The people used to sing her – Auntie Ivy. You see, she was from a different tribe. Auntie Ivy got very sick, and in the finish Grandpa got her back here to live with them.

Thomas Shadrack James and Con Edwards. (Courtesy Phillip Pepper)

'She had changed to a very fat woman. She never spoke and she didn't walk about, just sat on a high back chair all the time. She'd lean her arm on the back of the chair and rest her head there. Her hands were all puffy and her legs swollen. She ate hardly anything and she died after a year. They'd sung her.

'Now, the morning after she died when our family saw her, she was the same as the day she had left. Slender all over, her face beautiful again, and her hands and wrists were thin. It just happened overnight.

‘There was another daughter of my grandparents who was a wonderful dressmaker, but I don’t know which college she went to. She was beautiful, too. They were all clever, and they could all cook. Those James children all grew up on the Mission. Their son, Shadrach, was a wonderful man. I don’t know if he ever studied to be a lawyer, but if any dark person got into trouble round here he’d go to court for them. He knew the law inside out.

‘By the time Grandpa finished at Cumera, he had been everything there, even a great sportsman. There is a cricket cup in the family, a trophy. He captained the Cumera team and I believe they were premiers in the Echuca District Cricket Team.

Greg James and his mother, Roma, 1986.

‘There is the family story about him that at some time he had a surgery in Fitzroy. I know he lived there a long time ago. My cousin told me there was a brass plate on his gate with his name and degrees on it. She knows, because it was one of her chores every day to clean the brass. She often wonders where that brass plate is today. Our family also talks about his work with the Aspro Company and the development of some sort of medication that he was responsible for, but I don’t know any more than that. He was also supposed to have studied at the Sydney University.

‘I was a baby when we left Cumera in 1935 and we lived with

Grandma Ada and Grandpa at Maroopna, but that house was destroyed in a fire. We shifted to Shepparton and Grandpa opened a surgery, and he had that for many years. In fact, the first ten years of my life we lived with them. It seemed that Grandpa really clung to my father and, he more or less, ruled Dad's life, well, not exactly ruled him, but Grandpa James was the head of the family. He was a lay preacher earlier in his life and he continued this with prayer meetings every Thursday night, and on Sundays the few Aboriginal people who lived around here came to the house for a Church Meeting.

'Grandma Ada was a very quiet person and she never spoke about anybody. She never discussed her personal life. I can remember her when I was little, and her not saying much. It was always Grandpa who made all the decisions. She, sort of, kept a low profile. My Grandma always called him Mr James, and he called her Mrs James. She was an excellent cook and she did love meat. She would have it for breakfast, dinner and tea. He loved curry, naturally I suppose, being Indian. My Grandma would say to him, "Curry, curry, curry." He'd say to her then, "Yes, Mrs James, and meat, meat, meat, all the time and your insides are going to be red from all that meat."

'She had a nick-name for him that she used on Good Fridays. Grandpa was very strict about not eating meat on that one day of the year but Grandma just stayed the way she was. She loved meat! Every year she would deliberately cook him a big meat breakfast on Good Friday. He'd say to her, "We don't eat meat today, Mrs James," and she would get the Bible out and say to him, "There's the Bible, Mr Murphy. Now you show me where it says you can't eat meat." But he couldn't.

'That's where my father got his love of meat. Grandma always gave it to her family. This was when we lived in Shepparton where they had the surgery. Grandpa was well aware of the consumption danger and we were often treated by him with herbs and crushed powder. Grandma would never allow anything into the house from the surgery. She was frightened of tuberculosis, too, like Grandpa, and if any tea towels came in she destroyed them. If a cup appeared from the surgery she sent the girls outside with it to bung it to bits with the axe so that it could never be used in the house.

'After Grandma Ada and Grandpa James had died, my parents moved into their own home. Dad worked for Ardmona and stayed here, and got his long service leave. Aboriginal people can do well if they want to, if they work at it. Dad died in 1981. My mother was always called 'Nan James' by everyone and she was wonderful to the aboriginal community. Everybody loved her. She is dead, too.

'We had no hang-ups. We were told to get out and work, and we did. Everything we had, we worked for. If you want something you have to work for it and we've tried to pass that on to our children. They've all done well, and all worked hard. I feel we are a well adjusted family. I never judge people on what others say. I judge them on what I think they are.'

'Greg is a qualified builder,' Terry said. 'He got his certificate when he was twenty in 1979. He's teaching woodwork now.'

'Friends, mates, in general, they'll have a shot at you about Aboriginal jokes. You just laugh and carry on with them,' Greg said

'We are a family with a good sense of humour,' Roma laughed.

'If they keep it up, you can tell them some jokes, too. Call them milk shakes,' Greg grinned. 'Then you can follow that with by mentioning that our ancestors didn't have to steal a loaf of bread to get out to Australia.'

'Glen will get on the TV here and he'll have a joke, too, same sort of thing. We just laugh,' Terry said.

'People make jokes. I do, myself,' Roma said. 'When someone tells about a white person doing something, I've said things like, 'Blackfellows don't do that,' or 'Don't you know you can't kill Blackfellows with an axe?' Then they laugh.'

For a fleeting second Roma was serious. 'You know if someone's using a joke against you.' She offered me another cup of tea, poured a little hot water into her own, and waited while Terry filled her own cup and Greg's before she spoke again.

'Even in us there is a little bit of prejudice. Everyone's got a bit of prejudice. It may not be about colour. It could be about race, religion, anything. When I was growing up I never wanted to go out with an Italian boy, yet we had plenty of Italian friends. You see? Everyone has a bit of prejudice – if they're willing to admit it.'

Roma moved her cup across the table and stood up, a smile spreading across her face.

'In the summertime I enjoy telling my friends that I'm going home to get into my bikini so that I can get a nice suntan.'

Roma's family had certainly inherited her sense of humour.

In 1988, Greg was a member of the Bicentennial Australian Aboriginal Cricket Team which played in England as a tribute to the original Aboriginal Team that played there in 1868.

Chapter Fifteen

In Memory of

Sandy (John) Atkinson had told me not to miss visiting the Dharnya Cultural Centre so I was on the road again in 1986. The Centre is thirty-six kilometres from Echuca and located nine kilometres north of the Barmah township in the Barmah forest of redgums, yellow, black and grey box. However, it is the dharnya, the redgum, that is the survivor, the strong member of the forest. The Aboriginal Interpretative Centre has taken the Aboriginal word for red gum as its title. Established and supported by the Yotti Yotta community, the Department of Conservation, Forests and Lands, and the Shire of Nathalia. The purpose is to allow, and encourage, groups and individuals to learn the history of the area.

Mrs Denise Bulled, a descendant of the Yotti Yotta Morgan family was in charge of the Centre and I had an appointment to speak with her.

I crossed the bridge over the Murray River into Barmah, and followed the sign post direction, Moira Lakes Track, out of the town on a sealed road. It was late autumn and the brilliance of the sun slowly descending in the west glowed through the gum trees on Barmah Island, sending fiery flashes from the pink and red autumn-tinted leaves. Cockatoos and galahs screeched and screamed as they dodged through the trees. The levee banks, a reminder of the past, were constructed in the early days of settlement by white men to preserve their farming land from the regular seasonal flood waters. Here and there cattle munched and lumbered contentedly in the paddocks.

The narrow bitumen road suddenly disappeared in a cloud of misty dust, substituted with a corrugated, ruptured, dirt-billowing sandy track. As the forest tracks are usually graded, this was the only bad patch, and slowing right down gave the dust a chance to float away. The sun's rays filtered between the tree trunks throwing patterns of shade across the track which resembled the slats of venetian blinds.

At Rices Weir Bridge I entered the Barmah Forest over Broken Creek and continued ahead taking Sand Ridge Track which led to the Dharnya Centre. It also made its way well beyond the Centre through the red gum forest to Louie Atkinson's longed-for campsite, Thistle Bend, on the Murray.

The yearly muster of the stock grazing in the forest, had recently been completed and as I passed the muster yards I saw stacks of timber piled up, some already cut into logs. An information notice board announced, Barmah State Forest Conservation Forest and Lands. 'Barmah Forest. Cattle in this forest graze under agistment. Please do not disturb or harm them.'

Further along, old ringbarked trees stood mute. Facing them on the side of the track, a twisted, ancient tree held on to its birthplace, its white trunk stabbed with termite holes. High up on the trunk a Yotti Yotta man had removed the strong bark with a stone axe. The dead, spindly branches reached out grotesquely, the limbs stretched to their limit as though the tree had given up its soul in great torment and agony. I passed beneath its skeletal along the sandy track.

The surrounding forest was sparse at this point and the living trees were like old human beings in the latter stages of life, standing twisted and gnarled, leaning or doubled over; it seemed in respectful silence for their many dead companions about them.

The stands of majestic red gums were not too far away with their enormous but often short trunks and heavy branching limbs. How many fence posts, house stumps, wharves, railway sleepers and bridges had the forest given since the first red gum sawmill was established in Moama in 1856? Bullock wagons once hauled the gumtree logs to the bank of the river, there to be lashed to the barges as outriggers, and floated along the Murrray River to the mill.

The sight of the Dharnya Centre plunged the forest into the present. The three buildings which comprised the Centre were surrounded by well-kept green lawns. It is here that campers, visitors, tourists, and the curious, can receive information regarding the great Barmah Forest – the past, the present, and the expectations of the future.

A notice outside the main building announced this as,

> A project jointly sponsored by the Department of Conservation, forests and Lands, the local community and the employment programme, opened by the Minister, the Hon. Joan Kerner in December 1985.

Denise and I walked and talked.

'Before the centre was actually opened to the public the Yotti Yotta Land Council had the full use of it for a weekend and we all came out here and had a terrific weekend,' Denise told me. 'Yotti Yotta is pronounced in different ways. I've always thought it was Yotti Yotta, but I've always pronounced it, Yotti Yorta. Some say Yorti Yorta, or Yorta Yorta.'

As we entered the 'multi-purpose visitor centre' she pointed to a brass plaque on the wall which displayed the names of the working team.

'There were nine of our aboriginal men involved in building the complex. They were Bevan Atkinson, Neville Atkinson Christopher Firebrace, John Kerr, Anthony McGee, Trevor Nicholson, Anthony Russell, Graham Taylor, and Wallace Taylor.' Denise smiled. 'You'd know some of those names. The other men were Graeme Barclay, Michael Bell, James Bevis, Rex Dalphin, Maurie Downie, Peter Gaffy, Robin O'Flynn, Neil Richardson and John Rowe.'

As we moved into the hall a spectacular mural greets the visitors, depicting the creation of the Murray River. The text explained that during the creative period, ancestral beings moved across the earth creating the features of the tribal land. The most powerful being was Biami.

'Robin Bailey painted the mural. He is a descendant of the Cooper family.' The meaning of the figures in the painting can be followed by the words of the legend which are on show:

Biami sent his old lubra down out of the high country with her yam stick to dig for food. As she journeyed across the flat and waterless plains with her dogs, she had Biami's giant snake with her as he had sent it along to keep an eye on her. She walked for many weary miles, drawing a line in the sand with her yam stick, and behind her came the snake, sliding in and out of the line, making the curves of the river bed with his body. Then Biami spoke in a voice of thunder. Lightning flashed and rain fell and the water came flowing down the track the old woman and the snake had made. After many moons she came to the sea, and went to sleep in a cave while her dogs ran off and kicked up the sandhills about the river mouth.

'We have displays in this building that explain about the low lying areas of the red gum forest and how part of it began to die. There is a lot of material for people to see about the culture of the Aborigines as well.'

Denise's young son, Damien, walked with us across to the second building and as we neared it she said, 'Red gum and Murray pine timber was used in the construction of the camp's buildings. The bunkhouse can be hired by anyone when they come to enjoy the bush. It can take up to fifty-two people. There are bedrooms with four and six bunks in each. We've had a lot of school groups and there are more booked in. The Aboriginal co-operative at Echuca will be arranging a visit for the young one, and that should be interesting as a lot of those kids' background is here. The basic idea is to get them to be aware of who they are. It is important that the Aboriginal children know about the history of their own people. I hope my father will pass on to Damien the old stories and history, and the significance of places in the forest. It's important that the children should know'

The bunkhouse has showers and toilets. SEC power and a telephone. The third building is a kitchen-dining room with all facilities. The dining room doubles as a class room or recreation room.

'The Centre was used for a conference recently and we have had families staying here as well. As you'd expect, there are many people who come to the Barmah Forest during the holiday seasons and long weekends. Last Easter there were hundreds of campers along the river. We had sixty adults and children take part in a bush walk organised and run by Penny Richards. She is employed by the Education Department. Another of the activities was a camp fire and corroboree. That was popular. We had 300 attend that one.

I do the bush walks, pointing out the Aboriginal influence on the area. I show the people the plants and what they were used for by our people. There is another bush walk we have and that is for collecting bark for paintings. You see, my job mainly is to put the Aboriginal aspect into the programmes that are run by the Dharnya Centre. Sandra Bailey, a solicitor, is the co-ordinator for the Cumera co-operative. Sandra and Robin's mother was Elsie Cooper and lived at Cummeroogunga.'

The Dharnya Centre, 1986.

As we walked around the outside of the buildings Denise talked about an area in the forest where the tribal people had a battle. It lies loosely between War Creek and Cutting Creek next to Barmah Lake, and is named War Plain.

'Did you notice the muster paddock as you came in at Rice's Weir? Old Aaron Atkinson's hut was down there once. He lived in it for years, near the muster yards, but it has been moved closer to the Centre. We tell the visitors about the Old People and give them damper and billy tea around a campfire. We have walks at night looking for animals with a spotlight. Last night there were nine kangaroos just outside the Centre and three of them had joeys in their pouches. There is plenty of birdlife throughout the forest for visitors to see and lean about. Some day when we come back into the centre after having our lunch outside we even find them flying about in here.

The Leaning Canoe Tree.

The red gum forest began dying during the 193o's, so that was bad for the birds and animals and it was found the problem was because of irrigation as the Murray stayed too high. Where the land was low the red gums suffered. A lot has been done to stop that. Now we take the visitors to see the wetlands and the waterbirds.

The search for trees that have had the bark taken from them for shelters for the tribal people or for dishes, is rewarded when one is found.' Denise picked up a piece of bark lying on the lawn and twisted it in her fingers. 'There had been one old canoe tree found in the forest lately, but we found the bark was not taken with a stone axe but with steel implements.' She stopped talking and turned to me.

'It is a dead tree. Some people want to take it from the ground and place it near the Dharnya Centre. I believe it should be left where it is. That tree is part of the transition of our people. From the old way to the new.'

Denise Bulled and her son, Damien.

www.ingramcontent.com/pod-product-compliance
Ingram Content Group Australia Pty Ltd
76 Discovery Rd, Dandenong South VIC 3175, AU
AUHW020136130726
429791AU00003B/95

9 781925 333442